ABSTRACT

The overall aim of this study was to investigate the effect of public procurement contract determinants on organizational performance. The study followed descriptive study design and was guided by 4 objectives; to determine the effect of internal procurement processes on organizational performance, to assess the effect of policy/regulatory framework on organizational performance, to investigate the effect of leadership and management support on organizational performance, and to investigate the effect of ICT infrastructure support on organizational performance. The study followed a descriptive research design targeting the Nairobi County officials. With aid of 10 researcher assistants, the researcher and assistants targeted 87 finance procurement officers from Nairobi county government using semi-structured questionnaires, administered through drop and pick later method, and obtained 81 completed questionnaires - 93.10% response rate. The data was organized in excel spread sheets and analyzed using excel spread sheets and SPSS version 20. Regarding the effect of internal procurement processes on organizational performance, the sampled respondents stated that internal procurement processes do influence organizational performance majorly because procurement processes do enhance purchase quality, enhances controls in the organization, and manages possible self-interests, and increases efficiency and effectiveness. Regarding the effect of policy/regulatory framework on organizational performance, the respondents explained that policy and regulatory framework influences organizational performance because it creates a level playing field, shapes the environment for decision making, acts as a guide for the employees, upholds standards of quality and established parameters for monitoring and evaluation. Regarding the effect of leadership and management support on organizational performance, the respondents said that the procurement leadership and management does influence performance in their organization because; leaders are the custodians of morals in the organization, they provide direction to the organization, they ought to encourage and guide the junior officers to what is expected and are the main decision makers in an organization. Regarding the effect of ICT infrastructure support on organizational performance the respondents explained that ICT; enhances efficiency, monitoring and control, makes work easy, enhances communication and service delivery. The regression results regression results established a strong positive relationship between dependent variable organizational performance and the independent variables; Internal Procurement Processes, Regulatory Framework, Leadership and Management Support and ICT Infrastructure because the coefficient of determination (R) was 0.867 and correlation coefficient (R-Square) as 0.752. The study concludes that public procurement contract determinants do influence performance to a great extent. Organizations should eliminate inefficient and ineffective obstacles and challenges in the procurement process which cause wastage of resources and inhibit performance. Top leaders should cheer their team towards doing the right thing. Appropriate ICT infrastructure for procurement processes in bidding, technical and financial evaluation and monitoring should be supported by top leadership. Also, necessary structures to promote integrity and accountability should be upheld.

ACKNOWLEDGEMENT

First and foremost, I have to thank my late parents for their love and support throughout my life. Thank you both for giving me strength at times of need to reach the stars and chase my dreams. Indeed your divine prediction of me has come to pass. I take this opportunity to thank my supervisor Prof. Silas Onyango and Mr. George Ochiri for providing guidance on this project and being available for consultation whenever required. Special thanks to all those respondents who responded to the questionnaires. I also thank fellow colleagues for their words of encouragement and advice during the research period. My gratitude goes to my family who deserve whole hearted thanks for their support and understanding throughout the academic journey. Finally my sincere gratitude goes to my employer for having allowed me some time to attend class in pursuit of this degree program. Also, I sincerely thank the Almighty God for his provision.

TABLE OF CONTENTS

LIST OF TABLES AND FIGURES

AGP – Australian Government Policy

BCG – Boston Consulting Group

ICT- Information and Communication Technology

IFMIS- Integrated Financial Management Information System

IS- Information system

IT- Information Technology

KIPPRA - Kenya Institute for Public Policy Research and Analysis

KPI- Key Performance Indicators

KSF- Key success factor

PPDA-Public Procurement and Disposal Act

PPOA -Public Procurement Oversight Authority

SACCO- Savings and credit cooperative

SPSS- Statistical Package for Social Sciences

TOG – Technology and Outsourcing Group

TERMS AND DEFINITIONS

Internal Procurement Processes: Refer to the internal rules and regulations guidelines for procurement in organizations. Victor (2012) describes internal procurement regulations as lead indicators where management intervention is possible to affect customer and financial outcomes.

Policy Regulatory framework: The objectives of public procurement are implemented through various legal and regulatory framework within which policies relating to procurement and asset disposal are implemented (Del, 2008)

Leadership: Leadership refers to the ability to focus the progress of a group (Sharma, 2013)

Management: Management in businesses and organizations is the function that coordinates the efforts of people to accomplish goals and objectives by using available resources efficiently and effectively (Kariuki and Nzioki, 2010)

Leadership and Management support: Refer to the ability to negotiate for resources to achieve set goals in organizations. Peter (2011) defines leadership as executing planned tasks the right way

ICT Infrastructure Support: The medium in which, hardware, software and computer networking, internet and other support assists organizations in running efficiently (Kramer, 2007).

Contract Implementation: Refers to the migration and mobilization processes for organizations from contract negotiation to award (Spinney, 2007).

Policy Regulatory framework: Refer to the environment where objectives of public procurement are implemented through various regulations and policies relating to procurement and asset disposal (AGP, 2006).

Procurement: Refers to the acquisition of goods and or services at the best price that meets the needs of the purchaser in terms of quality, quantity, time, and location (Stephenson, 2009)

Procurement Strategy: Refers to a plan for optimizing external spend, procurement operations and other value contributions in a manner that supports the overall corporate agenda (RoK, 2010)

Wastage: Refers to the activities that do not add value leading to defects or rework of processes (Shigeo, 1981)

Organization Performance: Refers to determination of procurement performance bench marked on acceptable indicators (Tallur, 2008)

CHAPTER ONE

INTRODUCTION

1.1 Background to the study

Public procurement is a major instrument by which a government can encourage innovation in service delivery and drive the economy through savings. Procurement is perceived by tax payers as corruption designed to benefits few individuals at the expense of stakeholders. It is prone to wastage therefore affecting quality of service and organizational performance (Nzau and Njeru, 2014). There is need to reverse this worrying trend and win public confidence. The Government efforts to improve the procurement system still experience challenges on quality goods and services (Paul, 2011). Notably, the improper implementation of recommended performance standards within policy regulatory framework results in high operation costs, uncoordinated business activities, and failure to attract and retain professionals (Arrowsmith, 2010).

Nadiope (2005) defines a contract as a written or oral legally-binding agreement between the parties identified in the agreement to fulfill the terms and conditions outlined in the agreement. According to (Swinney, 2007), the prerequisite requirement for the enforcement of a contract, amongst other things, is the condition that the parties to the contract accept the terms of the claimed contract). Nzau and Njeru (2014) point out that historically, this was most commonly achieved through signature or performance, but in many jurisdictions – especially with the advance of electronic commerce - the forms of acceptance have expanded to include various forms of electronic signature (Victor, 2012). Contracts can be of many types; sales contracts (including leases), purchasing contracts, partnership agreements, trade agreements, and intellectual property agreements (Arrowsmith, 2010). According to Bailey (2008) Contract management is to ensure that all parties to the contract fulfill their contractual obligation. According to Porter (1985) contract life cycle management is the process of efficiently managing the contract creation, execution and analysis of maximizing operational and financial performance and minimizing risks. The ultimate goal of public procurement is to provide the required goods and services in time within set budgets (Errigde and Mcllroy, 2002). This ought to be complimented by effective contract management geared towards high organizational performance. Public entities should overcome existing challenges in order to enhance procurement processes that make a saving and avoid wastage. Ntayi (2009) in his study observes that millions of dollars get wasted in many countries due to inefficient and ineffective obstacles and challenges in the procurement process of which contract management is a part.

Kabaj (2003) contends that an efficient public procurement system may be a tool to pull African countries from poverty by saving on investments and utilize public resources to improve financial and non-financial performance. Rotich (2011) in a study on the factors affecting budget utilization in Kericho argued that organizations focus on their internal procurement process than other determinants such as policy regulatory framework, leadership and management support and ICT infrastructure support. He asserts that there is a tendency for organizations to concentrate on analyzing inputs and outputs ignoring processes.

Lenders (1997) in his study found that firms are reluctant to share information publicly because of competition. In a study undertaken by Nzau and Njeru (2014) on factors affecting procurement performance of public universities in Nairobi County found that organizations avoid disclosing procurement data to the public for privacy reasons (Nzau and Njeru, 2014).

Effective and efficient public procurement system can enhance financial and non-financial performance thus contributing immensely to Kenya's socioeconomic development in attaining the Vision 2030 Strategy (RoK$_2$, 2010).The strict implementation of procurement procedures is likely to eliminate weaknesses related to procurement operations and strict tendering security requirement constrained private sector access to public procurement. Chapter Twelve of The Constitution of Kenya, 2010, Part VI, has recognized the contribution of procurement to national economy. Public entities should contract in accordance with a system that is fair, equitable, transparent, competitive and cost effective (RoK$_3$, 2010).

Odhiambo and Kamau (2003) are categorical that procuring entities today are continuously facing external and internal problems when sourcing for their needs by the use of traditional procurement procedures. According to Nadiope (2003) problems such as poor information sharing between purchasers and suppliers, non-automated supplier appraisal systems, adversarial relationship and non-responsive supply chain integration exist in this electronic age.

1.1.1 Nairobi County

Nairobi County is one of the 47 counties in Kenya (Nzau and Njeru, 2014). Its capital is the City of Nairobi which is also the capital and largest city of Kenya. Nairobi was founded in 1899 by the colonial authorities in British East Africa, as a rail depot on the Uganda Railway. According to Mugambi and Theuri (2014) Nairobi is one of the most prominent cities in Africa, both politically and financially. The population of the county is estimated at about 3.36 million within 696 km^2.

The Nairobi County Government is charged with the responsibility of providing a variety of services to residents within its area of jurisdiction Nzau and Njeru (2014). In a study undertaken by Hagans (2013) on Livelihoods, land-use and public transport: Opportunities for poverty reduction and risks of splintering urbanism in Nairobi's Spatial Plans, established that services could be achieved through eight sectors; Lands Housing and Physical Planning, Health Services, Public Service Management, Public Works, Road and Transport, Education, Youth Affairs, culture and social services Inspectorate Services, Water, Energy, Forestry, Environment and Natural Resources and Trade, Industrialization, Corporate Development, Tourism and Wildlife sectors.

Murunga (2012) describes Nairobi County as the most cosmopolitan county government attractive to business investments therefore suitable for research. Some major contracts implemented include the construction of Thika Superhighway at a cost of KES 30 billion, the upgrading of Jomo Kenyatta international Airport at a cost of US $ 27.6 million. Pipeline contracts to be implemented include 100,000 housing units for residents, construction of overlay to ease congestion in the city from Likoni road to Westlands, the construction of 13km Outering road from North Airport road to Thika road at a cost of KES 8.5 and the implementation of a mass transport system in the city. Nairobi is the home of Safaricom limited, the largest mobile phone service provider with 20million subscribers, a market share of 67% and 3000 base stations across the country.

1.1.2 Procurement Contract

Trevor et al (2006) in a study on Managing Public Service Contracts: Aligning Values, Institutions, and Markets observes that a procurement contract is a legally enforceable mutual commitment of parties to deliver goods and services in a given policy legal framework. Some of challenges faced by procurement practitioners and managers in enforcing public service contracts is ensuring and improving the quality of goods and service delivery, exhibiting local leadership and management support in contracting activities, harmonizing local policy regulatory framework with international procurement processes, promotion of quality assurance of goods and services, preventing illegal conduct by promoting three procurement principles of fairness, competitiveness and transparency, and deterrent of political influence in contracting.

In practice, the degree to which leaders and managers can achieve values through delivery of goods services and influence organizational performance depends on commitment and positive attitude when undertaking activities within the organization. For instance some conditions such as external political influence, enforcement of policy regulatory framework and ICT infrastructure support lie beyond a manager's control without effective leadership and resources. For instance the delivery of goods and services with higher transaction costs pose greater contracting challenges in terms of leadership and management for organizations.

Designing contracts for a public entity is complex, requiring leadership and management support specifically in decision making at the beginning and during implementation. Some decisions undertaken before commencement of contracts include specifying the supplier's obligations and tasks, clauses in the contract in terms of contract amount, commencement, completion, amendment, compliance with government law, arbitration, termination, renewal provisions, and specifying incentive and performance-measurement systems.

The major challenge after awarding mega contracts lies in leadership and management support necessary in monitoring supplier performance, sharing progress with recipients, resolving conflicts and executing incentive programs under corporate social responsibility (Kelman, 2002). It is critical to identify and prioritize politically contentious issues and preferences by stakeholders before contract implementation in order to identify and manage external imposed constrains likely to affect the project. High public service performance require leadership and management support that goes beyond stakeholder's preferences and instead identification of new opportunities to enhance delivery of goods and services.

1.1.3 Organizational Performance

March and Sutton (2015) in a study on organizational performance as a dependent variable define organizational performance as dependent variable with identifiable variables that produce variation in performance. Organizations in the public sector should emulate good business practices to realize high performance. Business firms are compared in terms of profit, sales, market share, productivity, debt ratios and stock prices. BCG (2011) in a study on high performance organizations argues that continuous performance improvement should be the objective of organizations for growth. Gavrea et al (2011) in a study on determinants of organizational performance suggest that determinants enable to identify critical factors that can improve performance. In this study the determinants of organizational performance are described as: internal procurement processes, policy regulatory framework, leadership and management support and ICT infrastructure support.

It has been identified that assessing or determining organizational performance cannot be determined by merely assessing or analyzing the books of accounts. Unlike the past, verifying that the organization is performing at its best cannot be determined by simply identifying whether the organization is making profits or losses. If a firm makes huge profits at the expense of overworked employees, the form cannot be regarded as a high performing entity. Balancing effectiveness and efficiency if highly considered when determining organization performance.

Procurement must, therefore, be perceived as a fraction of a larger course in order to obtain the maximum output without compromising on the quality of processes and the satisfaction of the various stakeholders involved. Realizing the maximum output from the organisation propels the various parties to ensure that the right strategies and factors have been put in place. For instance, in order to obtain maximum organisation performance in relation to procurement, input focused, output focused, efficiency focused and effectiveness focused should all be considered (Australian Institute of Company Directors, 2015).

1.1.4. Procurement and Organizational Performance

Procurement determinants are diverse due to the various aspects of procurement (costs/pricing for example). In other scenarios, the determinants are influenced by the type of procurement in question, public procurement, for example, or the geographical location within which the procurement is taking place (the country). Procurement determinants can therefore be described as the factors influencing the outcome of procurement processes or the overall procurement performance. Various researchers have indicated various factors as determinants of procurement, whether in the public or private sector. Oluka and Basheka (2014) have on the determinants from a geographical location perspective, the focus being on Uganda. They indicate that the determinants present are contract management plans, defining processes clearly, clearly defined roles and a knowledgeable contract manager.

Alabano et al. (2008) also set to identify the determinants of contract management, the focus being on the Italian government. This research is set in relation to the determinants pertaining to geographical locations. Specifically, the researchers' attention is on the performance of suppliers on e-procurement. The researchers' identify that the firm's location, buyers' loyalty and MEPA negotiation tools have significantly facilitated the success of suppliers in e-procurement.

Hanlin (2011) got interested in identifying the how local procurement can be increased in the mining sector in the African region. The focus being on a specific sector, Hanlin (2011) identified that previous experiences, a disconnection between the mining companies and the local suppliers, centralized global procurement and precedent and risk aversion issues significantly impacted the increase or decrease of local procurement in the African region. Giancotti, Nardone and Rubba (2014) identify organizational determinants in procurement. Although the focus is on the medical arena, the researchers indicate some determinants that can be used to assess whether they are of any influence in the construction industry. The determinants include citizenship and social scenarios, clinical hospital organisation and organisation strategies scenarios.

The above mentioned researchers prove the previously made statement indicating that the determinants can vary depending on the industry, location or type of procurement made. For instance, e-procurement seems to be highly influenced by the technological as well as the ICT knowledge determinants. Somasundaram (2004) identifies that technological issues have highly influenced the attitudes of firms towards the adoption of e-procurement. Other influencers include competing electronic marketplaces and costly solutions. Hericksen et al. (2004) add that centralized solutions and purchasing power highly affect adoption attitudes in places such as Denmark. In other areas such as Norway, the lack of organizational change highly impacts adoption attitudes (Computerworld, 2004).

Although the determinants vary, it is evident that there are determinants which are recurring, regardless of the sector, geographical location or industry. For instance, the competence of the management appears to be a fundamental factor in procurement (Oluka and Basheka, 2014; Giancotti et al., 2014; Albao et al., 2008). In other researches, it has been identified that procurement processes (whether internal or external) have a significant role to play in determining procurement (Hericksen et al., 2004; Hanlin, 2011). Issues pertaining to the regulatory framework of a country or region as well as well as technological factors can also be traced in numerous researchers (Giancotti et al., 2014; Somasundaram, 2004).

According to Somasundaram (2004), organizational performance has over the years been categorized into three specific areas of outcomes of a firm. These includes; financial performance (profits, return on assets, return on investment), product market performance (sales, market share); and shareholder return (total shareholder return, economic value added). However, Richard et al. (2009) adds that various stakeholders have questioned the three approaches above which regards organizational performance as being just quantitative and neglects important aspects of financial performance. Kaplan and Norton (1992) brought the concept of balanced score card as being appropriate measure of organizational performance.

Upadhaya, Munir, and Blount (2014) holds that balanced score card is the most appropriate measure of performance since it incorporates measures related to; Financial, Customer, Internal business processes and Learning and growth aspects of an organization. This study used the concept of balanced score card to measure performance. The respondents were asked to give percentage rating of the extent to which public procurement contract determinants did influence the four aspects - Financial, Customer, Internal business processes and Learning and growth, in their organization over the year 2014. The percentage ratings for the four measures of performance were summed up and the average obtained as the measure of performance.

1.2 Statement of the problem

For public entities, Application of appropriate procurement processes, policy and frameworks, controls including use of modern technology, with proper support from senior management who are accountable to relevant authorities is essential are essential influencers of effectiveness or procurement function in an organization. For instance, Williamson (2000) argues that decline in performance in government entities results in poor delivery of goods and services. Public contract service is increasingly recognized as essential in service delivery (Kavua and Ngugi, 2014). Baquero (2005) argues that traditional government procurement contracts worldwide have tended to focus on internal procurement process rather than performance. In real sense the focus should be on the internal procurement processes, policy regulatory framework, ICT infrastructure support and leadership and management support to justify the quality and cost of projects. Notably, the traditional procurement contracts have been subject to abuse due to malpractices in the public sector. In Australia, Callender and Shapper (2003) in a study on public procurement reform established that public procurement is a major instrument by which a government can encourage innovation in service delivery and drive the economy.

Article 227 (RoK$_4$, 2010) requires public procurement systems to be fair, equitable, transparent, competitive and cost effective (RoK$_5$, 2010). The challenge is that the principles enshrined in the aforementioned article have not been enforced as expected under the regime of the Public Procurement and Disposal Act, 2005 (PPDA, 2005). Some of the weaknesses identified in the procurement contract implementation are failure to have fairness, competiveness and transparency as stipulated in section 227 of the constitution of Kenya (RoK$_5$, 2010). There is still lack of comprehensive internal procurement processes, policy regulatory framework, effective leadership and management and ICT infrastructure support. There is also lack of central body with technical expertise, absence of clearly defined rules and responsibilities for procurement entities and absence of comprehensive legal regime to safeguard public procurement, and monitor public procurement (Kinta, 2012). This means they may not be able to determine their efficiency and effectiveness (Victor, 2012).

Despite the importance of financial and non-financial evaluation of organizational performance researchers have inadequately paid attention to empirically and systematically pinpoint the procurement contract determinants and constraints by using objective 'hard data' (Jiang and Qureshi, 2006). In several countries, few articles have rigorously analyzed and empirically tested the factors that actually affect a government agency's decision to effectively manage procurement contracts (Nadiope, 2005). There is yet little or scarce empirical evidence on the effectiveness of procurement contract determinants specific to public procurement leading to excellent organizational performance (Boyne, 1998; Ferris and Graddy, 1986).

A review conducted by the PPOA, while recognizing some strength, identified a number of challenges including the cost of the procurement process, the long time to procure or reaction time to business opportunities, challenges of negotiation with suppliers, external approval processes and the issue of resale of branded items (PPOA, 2009). A research study is therefore needed to analyze and establish the best public procurement practices in commercial state owned enterprises because of the highlighted deficiencies. Further still, in spite of having various studies undertaken on procurement practices by various researchers, none of the studies have particularly addressed the effect of procurement contract determinants on performance of commercial state owned enterprises in Nairobi County. This has created a significant knowledge gap and therefore forms the basis for this study.

1.3 Main Objective

The purpose of this study was to investigate the effects of procurement contract determinants on the organizational performance

1.4 Specific Objectives

i) To determine the effect of internal procurement processes on organizational performance,

ii) To assess the effect of policy regulatory framework on organizational performance,

iii) To investigate effect of leadership and management support on organizational performance, and

iv) To investigate the effect of ICT infrastructure support on organizational performance.

1.5 Research Questions

i) To what extend does internal procurement process affect organizational performance?

ii) How does policy regulatory framework influence organizational performance?

iii) To what extend does leadership and management support affect organizational performance?

iv) How does ICT infrastructure support influence organizational performance?

1.6 Scope of the Study

The specific study variables of the study included internal procurement processes, procurement policy and regulatory frameworks, leadership and management support and support of ICT infrastructure. The study sought to establish how the above variables influence organizational performance. In this regard, the study conducted the literature review specifically related to the study variables. The data was obtained from the procurement officers or/and officers at the management level in a procurement department and specifically in a public institution or government agency. This is because procurement officers would provide relevant information. Also, government entity – specifically Nairobi County government, was targeted since the researcher sought to investigate the study variables in the context of public organization.

1.7 Significant of the Study

The findings of this study contribute to the body of literature in relation to the study topic. Future researchers on the topic; effect of contract determinants - internal procurement processes, procurement policy and regulatory frameworks, leadership and management support and support of ICT infrastructure, in relation to organizational performance can draw literatures from the study. Also, the study contributes to management and policy making in that the findings can help these professionals in making appropriate procurement environment for better contribution to organizational performance. Also, government agencies can draw from the study findings when designing procurement platforms and regulations so that public funds are effectively utilized in as far as procurement function is concerned. Also, legal practitioners and members of the public can draw important insights in relation to the study variables making them better informed to contribute to debates relating to procurement contract determinants and organizational performance.

CHAPTER TWO

LITERATURE REVIEW

2.1 Introduction

This chapter presents the past studies as well as theories related to determinants of public contracts. This review includes scholarly materials on current knowledge and substantial findings on procurement as well as theoretical and methodological contributions related to procurement contract implementation in the public sector. The chapter provides insight on the contract implementation which contributes to organization procurement performance.

2.2 Theoretical Framework

In this study, three theories, resource based theory Hegelian dialectic theory and systems theory, are reviewed. After discussing these theories, a theoretical framework is provided.

2.3 Resource Based Theory

Resource-based theory aspires to explain the internal sources of a firm's sustained competitive advantage (Kraaijenbrink, et al., 2010). It was Penrose who established the foundations of the resource-based view as a theory (RoosandRoos, 1997). The focus was mainly on efficient and innovative use of resources. It was identified that bundles of productive resources controlled by firms could vary significantly by firm, that firms in this sense are fundamentally heterogeneous even if they are in the same industry (Barney and Clark, 2007). Sandholm (2006) took on a resource perspective to analyze the role of procurement in new products development and ultimately organizational performance. Organizations diversify based on available resources and continue to accumulate through acquisition behaviors. This theory is relevant to independent variables in the study; internal procurement regulations, policy regulatory framework, leadership

15

and management and ICT infrastructure support due to available capacity and resources (spiller, 2008). Murunga et al (2012) in their study argue that to perform is to produce valued results. A performer can be an individual or a group of people engaging in a collaborative effort (Bartik, 2009). Developing organization procurement performance is a journey, and level of performance describes location in the journey (Apiyo and Mburu, 2014). The development of a procurement strategic plan for County governments with a clear vision and mission based on a business model is critical in enhancing organizational performance.

2.3.1 Resource Based Model: Input-Transformation-Output

Globally Organizations have potential to create markets for goods and services or shift their paradigm to have competitive advantage over others by effectively utilizing available resources to create new opportunities.

In a study undertaken by Grant (2001) on the resource based theory of competitive advantage it was found that resources are the inputs to the transformation process in an organization. Lee (2007) in a study on impacts of organization resources on agency performance describes resources in terms of qualified staff, budgets, enabling environment, information technology, specific intellectual property and others. Operations require coordination and use of resources. Capabilities are 'the capacity of a team to perform some task' (Grant, 2001). Resources are the source of capabilities – capabilities are the source of competitive edge. Markets can be created or paradigms changed by an organizations to its favor by use of the resources it has at its disposal to create new opportunities to enhance performance (Idris et al, 2011).

FIGURE 1

Resource Based Model: Input-Transformation

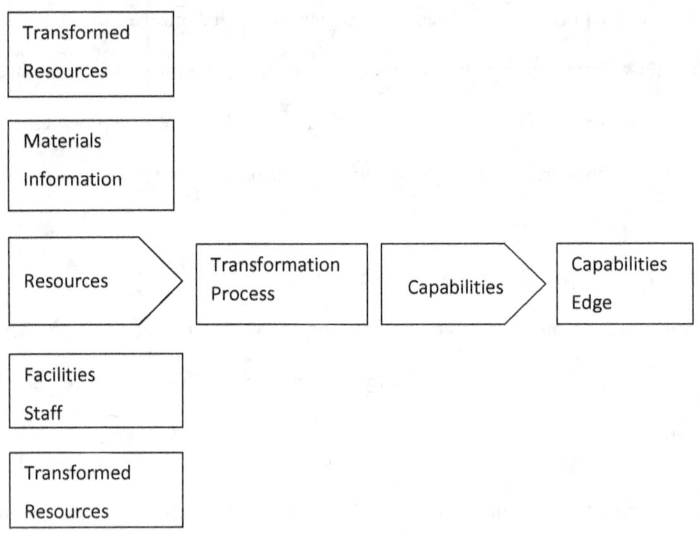

Source: Morgan (2010)

2.4 Hegelian Dialectic Theory

This study is based on Hegelian dialectic theory (Hegel, 1995). The theory has it that the organizational entity exists in a pluralistic world of colliding events, forces, or contradictory values that compete with each other for domination and control. Barney and Clark (2007) explain that change in organizations occurs when opposing values, forces or events gain sufficient power to confront and engage the status quo.

Jensen and Meckling (1976) agree that opposing forces are termed thesis (status-quo) and antithesis (new situation).

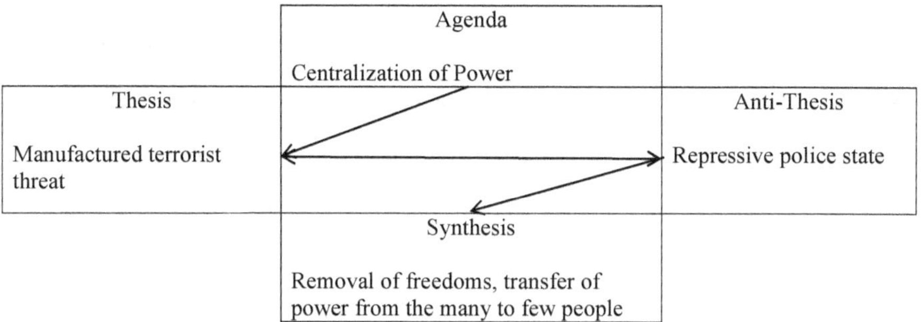

Source: Jones (2013)

This theory is applicable in the public sector when implementing changes in ICT infrastructure support, leadership and management support structures and internal procurement processes necessary in enhancing organizational performance (Victor, 2012). Rahim (2010) in a study on managing conflict in organizations contends that organizations need to learn and continuously change to improve their competitive positions. In a study undertaken by Lawler (2000) on designing change capable organization, it was found that change whether internal or external is associated with conflict and dealing with conflict is essential for realizing good performance.

In a study undertaken by Kazimoto (2013) on analysis of conflict management and leadership for organizational change, it was observed that leadership involves defining and communicating an organization's long-term vision and mission. A leader is someone who uses his or her influence to improve his organization managing conflict and change (Abbas and Asghar, 2010). Conflict management involves implementing strategies to limit the negative aspects of conflict and to increase the positive aspects of conflict, such as through enhanced team learning and group outcomes.

Childress (2009) in a study on leadership behavior and organizational performance pinpoints that quality leadership teams understand that their collective and individual behavior influences organizational performance. In a review by ADB (2014) on procurement policy, procedures and process, it was observed that procurement procedures of public sector competitive process must be subject to an independent internal review periodically within the legal and policy framework of the national government county. Victor (2012) observed that in order for organizations to remain competitive in procurement contract implementation, regulatory reform is necessary to adapt to market transition systems, new technologies and services to safeguard public interests.

2.5 Systems Theory

The systems theory established in 1968 by Ludwig Von Bertalanffy provides inside view of organizations. Ludwig argued that system theory focused on the study of organization activities that lead to high performance. Andras and Charlton (2005) in their finding argued that organizational ownership is collective responsibility bottom up. Systems theory provides an analytical framework for viewing the activities of an organization. Hatch and Cunliffe (2006) argued that leadership and management support recognize how system theory shapes a working environment for organization staff. Thomson (2007) in a study on supplier selection methods in public institutions assert that a procurement supply chain network is critical in realizing organizational goal. Hawthorne (2013) in a study on management theories and concepts at the workplace pinpoint that systems theory is instrumental for leadership and management support to examine activities at workplace. This theory could help leadership and management support in public entities to collectively monitor events in the entire organization with a view of identifying and isolating bottlenecks that could hinder program coordination (Hawthorne, 2013).

Systems theoretic analysis suggests that charismatic leadership and management support may improve organization financial and non-financial performance are likely to inject innovations into the internal rules within policy regulatory framework (Abbas, 2010). The charismatic leadership is useful on the short-term basis it is also a catalyst for long-term organizational performance (Goleman, 2004). Systems theory analysts argue that introduction and implementation of effective changes in the performance of organizations takes time to mature.

A system adaptive standardization of processes such as compatibility of internal rules with policy regulatory framework, leadership and management support and ICT infrastructure may lead to a shrinking of the system in the short-term. This implies that standardization reduces the complexity of internal and external procedures of organizations, leading to increase efficiency, effective use of resources and lead to performance improvement (Zaleznik, 2004).

In an interactive system, an entry moves towards a goal. In this study, procurement contract determinants constitute inputs, processes, and environment leading to the final state which is organizational performance. The inputs have to be transformed into inputs by a process (Salem, 2003).

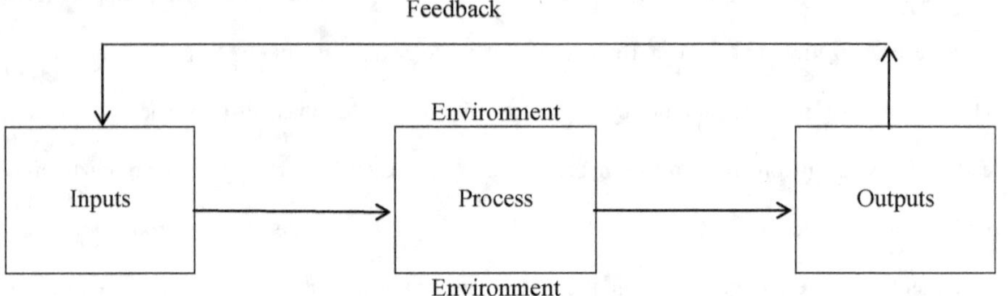

Source: Austin (1996)

The conceptual framework in figure 2.4 shows the relationship between the study variables. Independent variables, which are of procurement contract determinants constituted the activities carried out to support organizational performance. Independent variables include internal procurement process, policy regulatory framework, leadership and management support and ICT infrastructure support. Organizational performance is dependent variable in this study.

2.6 Empirical Literature

The prescriptive literature on procurement determinants tends to offer step-by-step procedures for procurement managers and other stakeholders in implementing contracts. In order for procurement contract to be implemented successfully parties involved ought to understand the provisions given in the document (Sanders, *et al.,* 2007; Laratta (2009) and Saunders, 2000). Successful and efficient contract management practices are those that meet the needs of the company's stakeholders, ensure rational and efficient of funds available, allow competition and manage the risk and potential liabilities to the buyer. Thus enforcement of existing internal procurement processes within the national policy regulatory framework measures must be enforced to enhance organizational performance.

Procurement practitioners ought to play a vital role in ensuring that the company's contractual obligations are fully achieved at the minimum cost possible. It is important for concerned parties to address the questions in the procurement contract through negotiation to flexibility especially delivery or completion date lines to avoid the risk due to demand uncertainty (Golovachkina and Bradley, 2002). But this is not usually the case as supported by Nadiope (2005) who observes that the government lacks trained procurement personnel. In an effort to attain these demands, organizations constantly look for employees who have skills necessary to deal with the wide variety of tasks (Monczka*et al.,* 1998; Sauber et al., 2008). Notwithstanding the above, Lan, *et al.,* (2005) posit that finding, hiring and retaining dedicated, energetic, and ethical employees with special skills is always hard. The supervisors (contract managers) should be knowledgeable in contract management. Organizations must, therefore, assign experienced staff to supervise the consultant and contractors. This should be accompanied by proper record keeping.

The obtainment of development undertaking is endless in extension in light of the fact that it includes the social occasion and sorting out of bunches of discrete people, firms and organizations to plan, oversee and fabricate development items, for example, houses, office structures, shopping complex, streets, spans and so on for specific clients or "customers". Procurement comes the word procure which literally means "to obtain by care or effort"; "to bring about" and "to acquire" (Masterman, 1996).

System is about "organized method, approach, technique, process or procedure". In this connection, venture acquirement is all that much worried with the sorted out systems or procedure and methodology of getting or securing a development item, for example, a house, shopping complex or street and wharf. It likewise includes orchestrating and organizing individuals to accomplish endorsed objectives or destinations. The Aqua Group (1999) portrayed acquisition as the procedure of getting or procuring products and administrations from another for some thought. Masterman (1996) depicted task acquirement as the hierarchical structure expected to outline and manufacture development ventures for a particular customer. It is as it were genuine in light of the fact that the procedure of "getting" a building by a customer includes a gathering of individuals who are united and sorted out deliberately in term of their parts, obligations, obligations and interrelationship between them.

Today, there are a few sorts or varieties of task acquisition frameworks being generally utilized as a part of the development business. They run from the customary framework to the numerous varieties of "fast-tracking" frameworks, for example, turnkey, outline and construct, assemble work exchange, administration contracting, and expense in addition to contracting and so on. The presentation of numerous varieties of venture acquirement framework was impelled by the journey for more effective and speedier venture conveyance framework and better venture execution (Murdoch and Hughes, 2000). They are advancements to the conventional conveyance technique went for taking care of the hanging demand of customers or clients. The diverse acquirement frameworks present have conveyed changes not just to the procedure and method of task conveyance additionally the parts of administration and association.

As specified prior, the presentation of distinctive "optimizing" task acquirement frameworks is the endeavor by the business to give better arrangement to its customers or clients, who are progressively demanding for "better esteem for cash" from their ventures in term of expense, time and quality. The distinctive undertaking acquirement frameworks present diverse systems, procedure and methodology of planning and development of tasks for the customer. These diverse frameworks additionally recommend the variety of the authoritative structure of the task groups in term of part, obligation and power. So how do the diverse acquisition frameworks influence the task execution given that the technique, procedure, method and association differ as indicated by the frameworks? This paper takes a gander at the diverse acquirement frameworks and their traits and how each of them influences the venture execution. There are numerous obtainment frameworks, as will be highlighted later, being utilized as a part of the development business now days. However the emphasis is just on the kind of acquisition frameworks that ordinarily utilized as a part of Malaysia now days i.e. conventional framework; plan and fabricate technique, administration contracting strategy and expert development administration system. The parameters for the measurement of project performance are many, but in this case consideration is given to only three elements – time, including speed of delivery, cost and quality.

Cost, time and quality are the three most important parameters of project performance. It has been stressed that in today's highly competitive and uncertain business environment, clients are demanding for better value from their investment. They want their project to be completed on time, within the estimated cost and with the right quality. The use of the various project procurement systems shows that the construction industry is now trying to meet the clients' needs (Chitkara, 2005). This is because the different procurement method will have different effect on the cost, time and quality of the project. Each project procurement system has its own peculiarity in term of the pretender and post tender activities and processes, division of risks between client and contractors, and the effectiveness of project monitoring and control. It is very important at the very outset of the project to carefully consider all factors when selecting the most appropriate procurement approach for a construction project. This is because each system has its own feature and peculiarity that will have effect on the cost, time and quality of the project i.e. the project performance.

2.6.1 Internal procurement processes

Procurement contract implementation in public institutions has, been overshadowed negatively due perceived inefficiency, corruption and disregard of value addition (PPDA, 2010). This has adversely impacted the rate and quality of progress in realizing the objectives of county development (Tan *et al.*, 2009). Effective policy regulatory framework could prevent employees from engaging in dishonest or unethical actions. As a public employee, you might have access to procurement and other nonpublic information that could affect a contract bid or the award process (Wymer and Regan, 2005). Improper disclosure of such protected information could violate numerous laws, as well as ethics rules. It also could subject you to administrative actions, as well as civil or criminal penalties. Salem(2003) in his findings argue that management in contracting authorities should ensure that good practice in purchasing and that procedures are followed to ensure compliance with all relevant guidelines. Tan et al (2009) describe internal procurement processes lead indicators where management intervention is possible to affect customer service and financial outcomes. Management theorist Drucker (2011) in his study on management practices believes that process improvements transform business and lead to innovation and represent "the change that creates a new dimension of performance" for organizations (Jordan and Young, 2008). In a study undertaken by Muhochi *et al.*, (2010) on opportunities and challenges of Business Process Management (BPM), points out that effective implementation and control of internal procurement processes enhance organization financial outcomes.

In Russia, a study undertaken by Becker and Martizner (2012) on promoting business process management excellence agrees that BPM is an effective methodology to use in times of crisis to make certain that the processes are efficient and effective, as this will result in a better and more cost efficient organization. Drucker (2011) points out that BPM empowers companies to align internal procurement processes that provide more value to both internal and external customers. Lardenoije, van Raaij and van Weele (2005) asserted that focusing on financial and neglecting non-financial performance cannot improve the procurement operations because only partial performance is considered.

Smith and Conway (1993) identified seven key success factors which influence procurement, namely; a clear procurement strategy, effective management information and control systems, development of expertise, role in corporate management, an entrepreneurial and proactive approach, co-ordination and focused efforts. An eighth is fundamental; communicate the key success factors to all levels of the organization and set out a procurement strategy to achieve continuous improvement in value for money (Abbas and Aghar, 2010). In understanding the procurement processes, it is possible to estimate the real cost involved with purchasing goods and services (Baily *et al.*, 2004).

Callender and Schapper (2003) in a study on public procurement in Australia assert that realization of procurement goals is influenced by internal and external forces. Gavrea et al., (2011) in their findings point out that interactions between various elements; professionalism, staffing levels and budget resources, procurement organizational structure, regulations, rules, and guidance, and internal control policies, all need attention and influence procurement performance (BCG, 2011). Benchmarking helps identify current best practice and then focuses on how internal processes could be re-engineered and managed to achieve excellence in critical procurement areas. Van Weele (2006) maintained that there is a link between internal procurement regulations, efficiency, effectiveness and performance. March and Sutton (2015) argue that high performance by organizations is an indication of progress towards set objectives, identifies areas of strengths and weaknesses and predicts the future.

In a study undertaken by Mugambi and Theuri (2014) on the challenges encountered by county governments in Kenya during budget preparation empirically examined the relationship between public participation in county budget preparation process and found no significant relationship between the independent and dependent variable. Similarly Rotich and Ngahu (2015) in a study on factors affecting budget utilization in Kericho county government identified tax compliance, vat policy, government policy and inflation effects as independent variables and budget utilization as dependent variable. They found no positive relationship between all independent variables and dependent variable. World Bank (2007) in a study on local budgeting argues that budget process and execution for local governments should be incorporated into managerial decision making continuously and management information incorporated in budget execution reporting.

Achieving efficiency in public procurement is an ambitious task, as procurement faces numerous challenges, especially due to the market structure, the legal framework and the political environment that procurers face (Thai, 2004). Pegnato (2003) estimated United States federal procurement at around $200 billion per annum, and Coggburn (2003) put the combined procurement for state and local governments at more than $1 trillion. Thai (2003) estimated government's collective purchasing at around 20 percent of Gross Domestic Product (GDP), and for developing countries, Nicol (2003) put the figure at 15 percent of GDP. For Russia, federal procurement in 2004 was expected to amount to about 40 percent of the country's budget (Fradkov, 2004).

The Organization for Economic Co-operation and Development (OECD), Development Assistance Committee (DAC) (2006) estimated the volume of global public sector procurement at 8 percent ($3.2 trillion) of the worldwide GDP of $40 trillion. The African public sector has been grappling with poverty and provision of effective services. Tackling the poverty challenge is the responsibility of the public sector in collaboration with other stakeholders. However, the state will deliver more effectively to all citizens and to poor people in particular if certain mechanisms are in place to man the running of government operations.

Public procurement in developing countries is said to account for up to 25 percent of their GDP. For a number of years the rate in industrialized countries has remained at around 10 percent. Though in absolute terms, the procurement market trade volume in developing countries may not be significant, the relative higher ratio it has on total GDP is an incentive big enough for formation of any economic alliance which most international trade organizations would not afford to easily let go, this is besides also the political impact it may pose (Arrowsmith, 2010). In the Middle East and Africa in general, central government purchases range from 9 to 13 percent (Gul, 2010). This indicates that public procurement plays a vital role in a country (Odhiambo and Kamau, 2003).

Public procurement therefore has important economic and political implications, and ensuring that the process is economical and efficient is crucial. This requires in part that the whole procurement process should be well understood by the actors: government, the procuring entities and the business community or suppliers and other stakeholders, including professional associations, academic entities and the general public.

While the Public Procurement and Disposal Act, 2005 was meant to address the challenges identified, experience suggests that the results have not entirely been as expected. The Public Procurement Act is important in the way the procurement processes are managed, and has sought to minimize cases of interference from players outside the concerned committees while at the same time discouraging fraudulent practices through debarment, transfer of procurements to other procuring entities and introduction of deterrent penalties. Article 227 of the Constitution of Kenya, 2010 has established a new framework to guide the public procurement and disposal process, which looks into ensuring that the Government Owned entities are agile enough to respond to opportunities in the market to grow value for the Kenyan public (RoK, 2010).

A review conducted by the PPOA, while recognizing some strength, identified a number of challenges including the cost of the procurement process, the long time to procure or reaction time to business opportunities, challenges of negotiation with suppliers, external approval processes and the issue of resale of branded items (PPOA, 2009). A research study is therefore needed to analyze and establish the best public procurement practices in commercial state owned enterprises because of the highlighted deficiencies. Further still, in spite of having various studies undertaken on procurement practices by various researchers, none of the studies have particularly addressed the effect of procurement practices on performance of commercial state owned enterprises in Nairobi County. This has created a significant knowledge gap and therefore forms the basis for this study.

2.6.2 Policy regulatory framework

Policies, laws, regulations and guidelines that provide procedures followed when implementing procurement contracts (AGP, 2006). The public procurement regulatory framework dictates that contracts must be drawn carefully involving all stakeholders for completeness so as to avoid unnecessary deviations (ROK_5, 2010). Minahan (2007) in his findings observes that it is possible to design public contracts that are robust within government policy regulatory framework to enhance organizational performance. This study identified four public contract determinants as internal procurement process, policy regulatory frameworks, leadership and management and ICT infrastructure support.

In a study undertaken by Spiller (2008) on Institution theory of public contracts argues that compliance with applicable obligations can enhance procurement practice. In a study undertaken by Victor (2012) on procurement policies in public procurement, found that the implementation of enhanced Institutional framework and management capacity for mainstreaming and integration into the public financial management system was long overdue. Apiyo and Mburu (2014) in a study on factors affecting procurement planning in county governments in Kenya found that creating a functional management or regulatory body and strengthening the institutional development capacity had a bearing on organizational performance.

In Australia Callender and Schapper (2003) in their findings on public procurement reform, found out that it was necessary for governments to enhance efficient procurement operations and practices. In addition Arthur (2009) points out that, enforcement of the public procurement market and putting in place efficient and effective contract administration and dispute resolution provisions reforms are necessary for the national and county governments (PPDA, 2010). In addition, Callender and Schapper (2003) argue that other reforms include safeguarding the integrity of the procurement system by establishing and enhancing control and audit system. In a study undertaken by Maiyo (2009) on irregularities in undertaking procurement practices in public institutions, it was found out that the entrenchment of efficient appeals mechanisms in the procurement policy was critical in fighting irregularities in public procurement. In addition Ongore and K'Obonyo (2011) pinpoint that introducing ethics and anticorruption measures in public procurement regulations was long overdue. Implementation of policy regulatory framework infrastructure can impact on the performance outcome.

Enforcement is viewed as any actions taken by regulators to ensure compliance (Zubcic and Sims, 2011). There are mixed opinions regarding the effect of enforcement on compliance. Sparrow (2000), argues that enforcement may make violators more sophisticated in how to prevent, and conceal detection by the authorities. However, Imperato (2005) agrees that enforcement improves compliance. According to Zubcic and Sims (2011), enforcement action and increased penalties lead to greater levels of compliance with laws. Corruption among government procurement officials in developing countries has been linked to a weak enforcement of the rule of law (Raymond, 2008).

In countries with complaint and review mechanisms, bidders are allowed to verify whether the procurement processes conform to the prescribed procedures. The possibility of review is also a strong incentive for procurement officials to abide by the rules (Hui et al., 2011). Public entities might choose to implement ineffective compliance systems if legal violations may be profitable in cases where the legal system under-enforces, either because penalties are set too low or because detection is imperfect or ineffective. Gunningham and Kagan, (2005) argue that the threat of legal sanctions is essential to regulatory compliance and that enforcement action has a cumulative effect on the consciousness of regulated organizations, and it reminds PEs and individuals that violators will be punished and to check their own compliance programs.

2.6.3 Leadership and Management support

Leaders will have a vision of what can be achieved and then communicate this to others and evolve strategies for realizing the vision (Abbas and Asghar, 2010). They motivate people and are able to negotiate for resources and other support to achieve their goals (Were *et al.,* 2012). In Australia , Kariuki and Nzioki (2010) in a study on the management of corporate Real Estate Asset in Kenya argue that it is the responsibility of managers to ensure that the available resources are well organized and applied to produce the best results. In the resource constrained and difficult environments a manager must also be a leader to achieve optimum results (Abbas and Asghar, 2010).

In a study undertaken by Epstein (2005), leadership was conceptualized in terms of commitment by the top management in evaluating its position regarding electronic business transactions. This was necessary for significant financial investment which must make resources available and cultural transformation to ensure culture orientation in an organization (Sharma and Jain, 2013). In the study undertaken by Jones (2004) the owners and managers need to be enthusiastic, passionate and firm believers in the benefits of electronic commerce. The study done by (Rashid and Al-Qirim, 2001), established that leadership and management are critical in contract implementation.

Abbas and Asghar (2010) in their finding argue that human actors are confronted with numerous challenges to adapt to unpredictable changes introduced in an organization to enhance performance. This may result in costly contractual breakdowns impacting negatively on organizational performance. When procurement contracts are managed well, resulting in high financial and non-financial performance then process ownership is realized with payoffs and costless bargaining is assumed (TOG, 2009). However, Kreps and Wilson (1982) and Williamson (2000) argue that failure to procedurally adhere to contractual obligation that factor determinants negatively affect performance. Non-verifiable problems that affect procurement function both internally and externally ought to be isolated and. Contracting proponents, whose roots are in economics, argue that effective implementation of procurement contract reduces service costs through competitive efficiencies and economies of scale enhancing organizational performance (Brown, et al., 2006).

Lack of a cadre of skilled professionals in public procurement is a major challenge that requires attention for national and county governments. Muge (2009) in a study on Procurement practice in public sector institutions in Kenya argues that procurement professionals are recognized as being in short supply globally. Paul (2011) and Muge (2009) in a study on procurement policies in public corporation suggests that Kenya's shortage of procurement practitioners can be addressed through measures including formally recognizing procurement as a profession, making training readily available, identifying MCIPS as the required Kenya qualification and formulating a strategic plan for Long Term Skills training.

Mamiro (2010) in his findings argues that one of the major challenges in public procurement is lack of proper internal procurement processes, leadership and management structure, unrealistic budgets and inadequacy of skills of procurement practitioners. Similarly, Kakwezi and Nyeko (2010) argue that organizational performance is focused on non-financial rather than financial functions. They conclude in their findings that failure to establish performance of the procurement function for public entities can lead to inefficient, irregular and costly consequences to the organizational performance.

In a study undertaken by Jordan and Young (2008) on top management support it was found that top management support was the most important critical success factor in contract implementation. Abbas and Asghar (2010) in the study on the role of leadership in organizational change established a significant relationship between organizational change and leadership characterized with vision and innovation. Despite top management support importance in implementation of procurement planning activities, the commitment for procurement planning issues from top management is however inadequate Sandberg, 2007. In Eisenstein and Thompson (2006) survey on Chief Executive Officers perspectives on Supply Chain

Management, only 23 percent of the responding Chief Executive Officers were responsible for driving development and execution of contracts.

It is considered that a company's success is due to organizational performance, employee job satisfaction and employee affective commitment (Bass, Rigio, 2006; Drucker, 2007). Some researchers have suggested that leaders motivate and help their employees to be competitive by using effective leadership styles (Bass, Rigio, 2006; Luftman, 2004). Therefore, the leader's use of effective leadership styles is due to promote standards of excellence in the professional development of the members of the organization (La Rue, Childs, Larson, 2004). Effective leadership also involves motivation, management, inspiration, remuneration and analytical skills. When all these are present, the organizations record increased employee satisfaction that positively that positively influences the productivity and the profits. The positive effect of leadership on organizational performance was measured by some researchers (Sila, Ebrahimpour, 2005) through human resources (turnover rate and job performance), organizational effectiveness (cost and quality) and financial performance (market share, profit, and return on asset). To increase the organizational performance a leader must have the ability to promote creativity and innovation, stimulate the subordinates to challenge their own value systems and improve their individual performance. A number of studies on leadership styles (Bass, Riggio, 2006; Kouzes, Posner, 2007, Yukl, 2009) suggest that the practices of the transformational leadership have a positive impact on the organizational performance.

There is no general agreement in the literature on the criteria to be used in assessing the organizational performance (Bolman, Deal 2003; DeClerk, 2008; La Rue et al, 2004; Scott, Davis, 2007). However, there are four main dominant approaches: Goal Approach. People create organizations for a specific purpose which is determined by the stakeholders. The organizational performance is the ability of the organization to achieve its goals. This approach explores the relation between the organization and the environment. As Boman and Deal (2003) state an organization is performant and effective when it takes advantage of its environment in the acquisition of high value and scarce resources to endorse its operations. Constituency Approach, according to Agle, et al., (2006) an organization is effective when multiple stakeholders perceive the organization as effective. The organizations with more control over resources are likely to have the most influence on the performance (Scott, Davis, 2007). Competing Values Approach was developed by Cameron and Quinn (2006) and it states that organizational goals are created in different directions by the various expectations of multiple constituencies. Therefore, organizations may have different criteria to measure performance. According to Cameron and Quinn (2006) stakeholders support the adaptability of their organizations; they want them to be flexible, stable and effective. A performing and effective organization has a high degree of collaboration and commitment among stakeholders through work groups, team projects and management (Cohen and Bradford, 2005). For Scott, Davis (2007), the flexibility and the ability of the organization to take advantage of its environment in the acquisition of internal and external resources are indicators of performance, its value being measured by the stock market and it is the key metric to measuring organizational performance. Other means to increase organizational efficiency and effectiveness include strategic initiatives focused on organizational performance.

Information Technology (IT) is a general term that describes any technology that helps to produce, manipulate process, store, communicate, and/or disseminate information (William, 2005). Lucas (1987) defines an information system as a set of structured procedures which, when effected, gives information for decision making. In a study by Olson and Gordon (1998) an information system is an integrated user-machine system for providing information to support operations, management, analysis and decision making functions in an organization. From these three definitions, ICT can be viewed as the enabling system that facilitate the processing and flow of information as well as the technologies used in the actual processing that goes on to produce a product or to provide a service to customers.

Technology adoption research explains in almost all cases, particularly in network technologies ICT included, that S-shaped adoption curves can be observed. The diffusion of an innovation starts slowly with a few early adopters. Information technology makes easy communication between persons or groups who are not physically near the same locality (Raymond, 2005). Systems such as cell phone, telex, radio, television, and video conferencing are included, as well as more modern computer-based technologies.

Over the past decade, user adoption has risen at basically the same rate as the increase in suppliers enabled supply chain (Van Weel, 2006). With added products and suppliers on the procurement processes, users have fewer motives to try to outwit the system (Minihan, 2007). Still, end users report that quite a few factors continue to seize back user adoption; these include inadequate accounts of spending categories within the system coupled with unpredictable purchase requirements plus bureaucracy procedures and policies to drive adoption, and distorted supply bases (Raymond, 2005).

However best Practice firms have been working on user adoption for years, and many supply managers at these ventures have become top "sellers" of the ICT enabled procurement system to end users (Kramer et al., 2007). The study undertaken by Bako (1991) argues that inter-organizational information systems can play an important role in supporting the resulting bilateral relationship.

Liker and Choi (2004) also concluded that Toyota and Honda have built great supplier relationships by following six distinct steps: understanding how your suppliers work, turning supplier rivalry into opportunity, supervising your suppliers, developing supplier's technical capabilities, sharing information intensively but selectively, and conducting joint improvement activities(Kazimoto, 2013). This shows that some evidence for information sharing will impact partner relationship. Ellram (1995) also, in her study, found five key factors for establishing successful partnerships. These five key factors are: two-way information sharing, top management support, shared goals, early communication to suppliers and supplier adds distinctive value. We can see that information sharing can establish a successful partnership. Therefore, it can be expected that if firms enhance its information sharing ability, they are likely to strengthen their partner relationship.

In the study on the factors affecting procurement planning in county governments in Kenya, Apiyo and Mburu (2014) empirically examined the relationship between staff competence, top management support, ICT tools and budgeting procedure as independent variable and procurement planning as dependent variable. The findings of the study indicated positive relationship between independent variables and dependent variable. On the contrary, Nzau and Njeru (2014) analyzed the factors affecting procurement performance of public universities in Nairobi County by empirically examining the relationships between staff competence and top management as independent variables and procurement planning as dependent variable. By contrast their findings excluded ICT tools and budgeting procedure as independent variables. But staff competence and top management support as independent variables indicated a positive relationship with the dependent variable.

In a study undertaken by Kramer (2007) on the role of the information and communication technology sector in expanding economic opportunities defines ICT as the technology which supports activities relating to the design, storage, and transmission of data and voice, jointly with their interrelated methods. Based on this definition, ICT signifies the technological standpoint of an information system (IS) and comprise computing, telecommunications and automation activities. Many organizations have implemented the use of information and communication technology (ICT) in order to develop the products and services they offer to their customers in real time.

Integrated information systems (IS) have taken center stage in changing organizations. Today, IS have been adopted by several organizational to enhance financial and non-financial performance According to Kitur (2006) several organizations including banks, insurance companies, and service companies have adopted ICT and considers it as a key success factor (KSF) for the reason that it has turned out to be the motivating force that is decisive in the production and delivery of goods and services in those industries. The adoption of ICT infrastructure support significantly impact on efficiency and organizational performance.

In the study undertaken by Tan et al., (2002) on factors influencing the adoption of internet-based ICTs it was found that information sharing related to the use of IT was useful in determining customers' future need and participation in sourcing decision. Li et al., (2005) mentioned that information sharing refers to the extent to which critical and proprietary information is communicated to one's supply chain partner. From the description above, the information sharing does not only share information with partners, but also provides adequate, timely and accurate information. In other words, information sharing should include the concept of information quality. Information quality includes such aspects as the accuracy, timeliness, adequacy, and credibility of information exchanged (Monczka *et al.*, 1998). Lee *et al.*, (1997) had the example of the dysfunctional effects of inaccurate/delayed information, as information moves along the supply chain.

Hagen and Zeed (2005) in a study on the use of ICT for firm productivity argue that public institutions must utilize ICT effectively to enhance procurement processes within the regulatory framework. Abouzeeddan and Busler (2002) argue that ICT can enhance service delivery and improve internal efficiencies by lowering costs and increasing productivity. Information sharing thus includes both formal and informal information sharing with partners (Victor, 2012). And the information must ensure the quality with accuracy, timeliness, adequacy, credibility, and criticality (Croom, 2003). Ensuring the quality of shared information has become a critical issue of effective Supply Chain Management (Cagiano *et al.*, 2003), supported that internet or internet tool can facilitate information sharing and more collaboratively with their partners. E-procurement is a kind of internet tool in their article. Eng (2004) also said that e-marketplace provides a shared internet-based infrastructure that enables participant organizations to communicate with one another effortlessly. Presutti (2003) proposed that in the e-design stage, buyer and seller share information in real time to build specifications that add value to the resulting product. That communication helps to minimize design complexities and avoids building in unnecessary costs into the specification.

In the study on the factors affecting electronic procurement implementation in automobile industry in Kenya, Gakure and Kangogo (2013) empirically examined the relationships between organizational factors, management support, technical support and environment factors as independent variables and e-procurement implementation as dependent variable found that there is a positive relationship between all independent variables and dependent variable. Similarly Oketch (2014) confirmed that by conducting a study on implementation of government electronic procurement in system in the county of Mombasa by identifying lack of experienced personnel as hindrance for seamless transition from manual to electronic procurement environment. Similarly Orina (2013) identified finance, leadership, legal framework and competent staff as key factors in implementing e-procurement in the public sector.

In a study by Apiyo and Mburu (2014) the challenges identified in implementing e-procurement include lack of capacity building programs, ICT infrastructure and Internet readiness. The other challenge stated in the findings on interconnectivity between county governments and the treasury and has been resolved by the implementation of cross boarder solution dabbed IFMIS. According to both Dorotinsky (2003) and Rozner (2008), in Hendricks (2012) in a study undertaken on effective implementation by the public sector of South Africa, IFMIS was defined as an automated public financial management system that interlinks planning, budgeting, procurement, expenditure management and control, accounting, auditing and reporting.

National Treasury's IFMIS Department rolled out e-procurement in Ministries, Departments, Agencies and counties and works closely with the Public Procurement Oversight Authority to ensure full implementation (PPDA, 2005). This is contrary to the study undertaken by Orina (2013) that identified resistance to change as a major challenge in implementation of e-procurement in public sector.

Karanja and Ng'ang'a (2014) in a study on Factors Influencing Implementation of Integrated Financial Management Information System in Kenya Government Ministries, it was found that there was a significant relationship between financial managers and available technology. The study's findings found that a positive relationship exist between the independent variables and dependent variable. Full implementation of IFMIS will support leadership and management timely and required information for decision making (RoK$_6$, 2010).

In the study undertaken on procurement practices affecting effective public projects implementation in Kenya, Barasa (2014) empirically examined the relationship between procurement planning, contract monitoring and control, choice of procurement procedure and communication independent variables and effective project implementation as dependent variable and found that there was positive relationship between independent variables and dependent variable. This was affirmed by Ameya *et al.,* (2012) in Ghana who studied public procurement law by empirically examining the factors that prohibit smooth implementation of public procurement law. It was established that less competitive procurement methods were preferred due to lack of qualified personnel and integrated ICT infrastructure support.

In the study on the factors affecting implementation of public procurement Act in SACCO societies in Kenya closely related to the present study, Kiama (2014) empirically examined the relationship between strategic planning, regulation enforcement and organizational culture as independent variable and implementation of public procurement as dependent variable and found that there was positive relationship between independent and dependent variables. The findings could be different in other SACCOs given differences in organizational structures and regulations (PPDA, 2005). Similarly, Apiyo and Mburu (2014) analyzed the factors affecting implementation of public procurement planning in county Governments in Kenya focusing Nairobi County Government by empirically examining and establishing a positive relationship staff competence and procurement planning.

Over the past three decades, much research has investigated the influence of IT investments on productivity. A review of the IT-organizational performance literature reveals that the relationship between IT investment and organizational performance has been researched at three major levels: the country level (Dewan and Kraemer, 2000), the industry level (Jorgenson and Stiroh, 2000), and the firm level (Dewan and Min, 1997). As stated earlier, contrary to the conventional wisdom that investment in IT leads to higher productivity, studies conducted in the late 1980s and early 1990s failed to find evidence supporting this relationship (Jorgenson and Stiroh, 1995). The lack of evidence soon became known as the organizational productivity paradox; that is, results failing to show that spending on IT increased macroeconomic productivity, or as Robert Solow, the Nobel Laureate, stated, the computer age is everywhere but in the organizational performance statistics.

Brynjolfsson and Hitt (2003) attributed these perplexing results to the then small share of the economy that IT represented, an explanation echoed by Sichel (1997) who contended that IT capital stock was too small a portion of the total capital stock to have a substantial impact. At the time, aggregate US ICT capital investments as a share of total capital investment was less than 10% (Dedrick and Kraemer, 2003). Since then, US ICT capital investment as percentage of total capital investment has grown dramatically. Recent studies have found that US ICT investments have shown a positive effect on organizational performance and economic growth (Jorgenson and Stiroh, 2000; Jorgenson, 2001; Oliner and Sichel, 2000). For example, Jorgenson and Stiroh (2000) found that IT contributed about 13% of the 3.04% economic growth and 27% of the 1.4% labor organizational performance growth in the U.S during the period 1973-1995 (Dedrick and Kraemer, 2003).

Jorgenson (2001) found that IT investment contributed about 28% of the 4.08% economic growth and 42% of the 2.11% labor productivity growth in the U.S during the period 1995-1999 (Dedrick and Kraemer, 2003). Extending Brynjolfsson and Hitt (2003) logic, a possible explanation of the positive IT-organizational performance findings is the dramatic increase in IT capital investments as a share of total capital investments, which exploded in the 1990s, from 9% in 1990 to 33% in 2000. Examining aggregate data across 17 developed countries over the period 1985-1992, Dewan and Kaeramer (2000) found that these economies were earning a positive and significant return on their IT investments, concluding that IT investments are contributing to output and organizational performance at a rate that is disproportionate to their factor share in production.

Schreyer (1999) examined IT's contribution to productivity and economic growth for the Great seven countries during the period 1990-1996. He too found that IT made a positive contribution to productivity and economic growth in all of the G-7 countries over the years studied. These studies provide strong evidence that IT capital is now contributing to productivity and growth in developed countries which renders the productivity paradox as non-issue in developed countries. Collectively these and earlier studies also suggest that the organizational performance paradox may exist until ICT capital investment as a share of total capital investment approaches 33% as it did in 2000 in the US. This does not bode well for developing economies depending on investment in IT to improve productivity.

In addition to dispelling the organizational performance paradox, finding a positive and significant return on ICT capital investments for developed countries, Dewan and Kaeramer (2000) found that non-ICT capital investments were not commensurate with their share of total capital investment. Interestingly, they also found that the situation reversed for the developing countries in their studies, where the developing economies earned a significant return on their non-ICT capital but investments in ICT failed to show a return on investment an indication of the existence of organizational productivity paradox in developing countries. Two possible explanations were advanced as to why ICT failed to increase organizational performance in developing countries.

First, the insignificance of ICT contributions is attributed to the lack of resource complementarily, with the authors noting that "compared to the advanced countries, less developed countries have poorer infrastructure, inherently less productive human capital (in part due to lower levels of education) and business models that have yet to transition from the industrial to the information age" (Dewan and Kaeramer, 2000). In other words, countries, organizations, and individuals must acquire and accumulate a certain level of experience with technologies before they become proficient and investments in IT capital start to earn a return. A related explanation is the relatively low level of IT capital stock in developing countries to have a substantial economic impact - the situation that existed in developed countries until the 1990s. A review of the research on the relationship between IT investment and firm-level performance reveals two contrasting schools of thought.

The first school of thought, dominant until the early 1990's, took a myopic view of the relationship between performance and IT investments. According to this school, IT investments per se confer sustainable performance and create competitive advantage through perpetual innovation and early IT adoption (Porter and Millar, 1985). However, recent (early 1990s to date) evidence indicates that IT investments alone do not produce sustainable competitive advantages nor do they result in superior performance (Clemons, 1991; Kettinger et al., 1994).

Clemons (1991) and Kettinger et al. (1994) identify several reasons for differences in findings. In addition to methodology and sampling flaws, the pervasiveness of IT, the relative ease of acquiring IT in competitive markets, and the ease of imitating and duplicating IT resources have all been cited as possible reasons why IT alone has failed to show a measurable positive contribution to superior economic performance and sustainable competitive advantage. Another explanation, which is of special importance to this research, is offered by the resource-based view (RBV) theory, which was introduced into information systems research by Barney (1991). According to the RBV theory, firms hold heterogeneous resource portfolios- whether by history, accident, or design- and that this resource heterogeneity is responsible for observed variability in financial returns across firms. Combining the empirical evidence from the post-1990s studies of ICT macroeconomic performance with the logic of the RBV theory produces a new paradigm.

According to this perspective, organizations cannot expect IT alone to produce sustainable performance and/or competitive advantage. Rather, it is how organizations use their IT resources to leverage and exploit pre-existing complementary 22 resources that enables or inhibits superior performance and competitive advantage. As we shall see below, the work presented here draws on the RBV theory as a foundation for explaining the difference in K'T macroeconomic productivity and growth between developed and developing countries.

2.7 Critique

In the study on the factors affecting procurement planning in county governments in Kenya, Apiyo and Mburu (2014) empirically examined the relationship between staff competence, top management support, ICT tools and budgeting procedure as independent variable and procurement planning as dependent variable. The findings of the study indicated positive relationship between independent variables and dependent variable. On the contrary, Nzau and Njeru (2014) analyzed the factors affecting procurement performance of public universities in Nairobi County by empirically examining the relationships between staff competence and top management as independent variables and procurement planning as dependent variable. By contrast their findings excluded ICT infrastructure support and budgeting procedures

In a study by Barasa (2014), the challenges identified in implementing e-procurement include lack of capacity building programs, ICT infrastructure and Internet readiness. The other challenge stated in the findings on interconnectivity between county governments and the treasury and has been resolved by the implementation of cross boarder solution dabbed IFMIS. This is contrary to the study undertaken by Orina (2013) that identified resistance to change as a major challenge in implementation of e-procurement in public sector.

In a study undertaken by Mugambi and Theuri (2014) on the challenges encountered by county governments in Kenya during budget preparation empirically examined the relationship between public participation in county budget preparation process and found no significant relationship between the independent and dependent variable. Similarly Rotich and Ngahu (2015) in a study on factors affecting budget utilization in Kericho county government identified tax compliance, vat policy, government policy and inflation effects as independent variables and budget utilization as dependent variable. They found no positive relationship between all independent variables and dependent variable. The inclusion of internal processes as a determinant for procurement contract implementation is critical success factor in enhancing organization procurement performance.

In a study undertaken by Jordan and Young (2008) on top management support it was found that top management support was the most important critical success factor in contract implementation. Abbas and Asghar (2010) in the study on the role of leadership in organizational change established a significant relationship between organizational change and leadership characterized with vision and innovation. Sharma (2013) observes that despite the importance of top management support in implementation of procurement planning activities, the commitment for procurement planning issues from top management is however inadequate Sandberg, 2007. In Eisenstein and Thompson (2006) survey on Chief Executive Officers perspectives on Supply Chain Management, only 23 percent of the responding Chief Executive Officers were responsible for driving development and execution of contracts. Leadership and management is key in determining organization procurement performance.

2.8 Summary of Literature Review

Summary of the literature review gives the theoretical literature which included theories such as: Resource based theory, Hegelian dialect theory and system theory by linking them to the effects of procurement contract determinants and organizational performance as variables under study respectively. The conceptual framework shows the relationship between organizational performances as dependent variable with independent variables: internal procurement regulations, policy regulatory framework, leadership and management support and ICT infrastructure support. Empirical literature identified recent studies in this thematic area and a critique of the existing literature, which departs from the studies in the empirical literature with the present study that proposes to assess effects of procurement contract determinants on organizational performance.

2.9 Research Gap

In a study undertaken by Nzau and Njeru (2014) on factors affecting procurement performance of public universities in Nairobi by empirically examining the relationships between staff competence and top management as independent variables and procurement planning as dependent variable. By contrast their findings excluded ICT infrastructure and leadership management support, policy regulatory framework and organizational performance as variables. Sharma (2013) on Leadership Management it was observed that the commitment for procurement planning issues from top management within an organization was inadequate. The study failed to capture internal procurement regulation, ICT infrastructure support, organizational performance and policy regulatory framework as variables.

In Eisenstein and Thompson (2006) survey on Chief Executive Officers perspectives on Supply Chain Management, only 23 percent of the responding Chief Executive Officers were responsible for driving development and execution of contracts. The study failed to capture other variables as internal procurement processes, policy regulatory framework, ICT infrastructure support and organizational performance. Most recent studies on procurement contract implementation focus on regulations, compliance, information technology, management, corruption leaving a gap between procurement contract determinants; internal procurement processes, procurement policy and regulatory frameworks, leadership and management support and support of ICT infrastructure as influencers to organizational performance. This study evaluates the effects of procurement contract determinants on organizational performance.

2.9.1 Conceptual Framework

Saunders *et al* (2007) in their findings on research methods define conceptual framework as the identification of key concepts about a phenomenon and representation of relationships derived from observations. Reichel and Ramey (2011) defines conceptual framework as a set of broad ideas and principles taken from relevant fields of enquiry and used to structure a subsequent presentation. Below are the elements of the conceptual framework of this study.

Internal procurement Processes; they govern modalities of conducting purchase requests, development and implementation of budgets, defines and manages procurement quality and defines payment methods and to what accounts.

Policy and Regulatory Framework; governs the relationship between various actions by specific parties. They include internal relations, external relations and legal requirements that stipulate the steps and formalities that have to be adhered to.

Leadership and Management Support; professional qualifications of the individual, work experience and IT competence are essential ingredients to organizational performance.

ICT Infrastructure support; includes the hardware and software, networks, internets, intranets, employee competence to technology and implementation of tasks by an organization with an aim of better performance.

Organizational Performance; as measured using balanced score card parameters. They include a measure of financial, customer, internal business processes and learning and development aspects of an organization.

Conceptual Framework

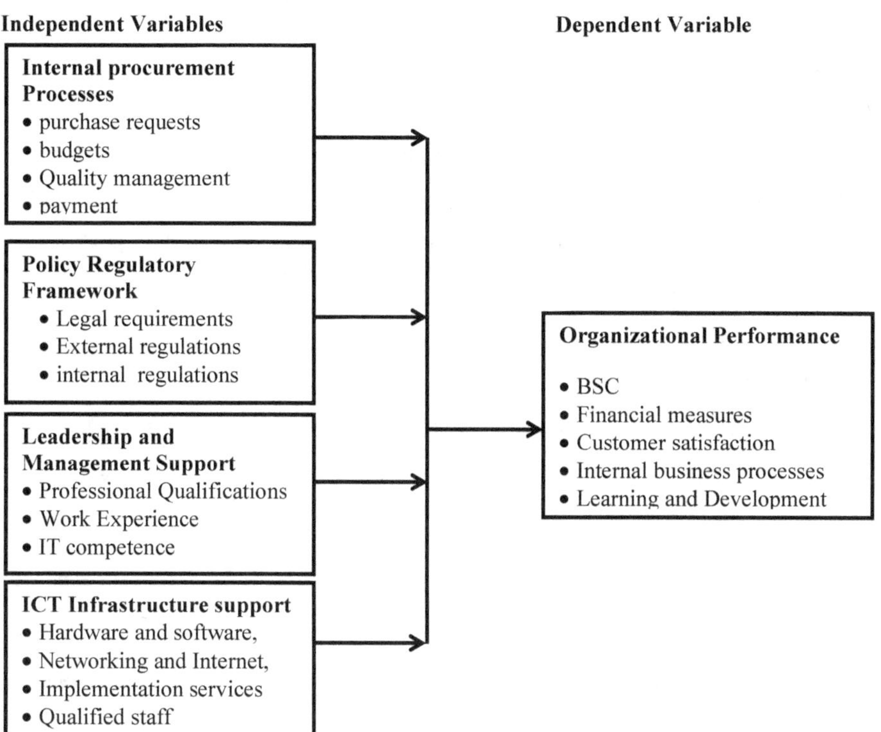

CHAPTER THREE

RESEARCH METHODOLOGY

3.1 Introduction

The chapter explains in details the methodology of the study including the research design, target population, sampling size, sampling technique, and procedures of data collection. The procedures and methodology adopted in the study to validate the outcome of the research are explained.

3.2 Research Philosophies

Research paradigm is presented in three distinct components. They are entomology, epistemology and methodology. In entomology, a researcher is compelled to follow common assumptions gathered in order to aid a researcher in understanding the reality of a society. When referring to epistemology, researchers are guided by common parameters and assumptions linked to excellent ways of investigating the real world's nature. Researchers guided by methodology follow a combination of procedures and methods in the assessment of diverse situations (Sekaran and Bougie, 2010).

Flowers (2009) indicate that a researcher must consider the various research paradigms and matters of ontology and epistemology when considering any research. The parameters considered delineate knowledge of the reality, perceptions, truth, nature of reality and assumptions. After considering these aspects, a researcher is able to know which method to adapt when at the design, sampling, data collections and analysis and conclusion phases of the research.

James and Vannicombe (2002) remind researchers that whereas they are unique and can be guided by their preferences and research objectives when choosing research methods, other issues have to be considered.

Blaikie (1993) posits that their preference should not overrule the distinct need of choosing the appropriate method for the research in question, amongst other issues, as a successful research must be characterized by articulated strategies that are well laid in order to meet the research's objectives. Blaikie (1993) reminds researchers that the "freewill" complex is introduced by humanistic elements, which may bring additional complexities. Nevertheless, Hatch and Cunliffe (2006) indicate that diverse paradigms propel the various researchers to embrace different ways in carrying out their research. These allow a researcher looking at a phenomenon through different perspectives to gain diverse kinds of knowledge.

The best techniques and procedures must be established when conducting a research in order to make acceptable conclusions in as far as the established assumptions are concerned. For instance, positivism unfolds some given truth in a phenomenon. A suitable structured approach must therefore be embraced. This should be carried out with a combination of empirical observations and logical deductions that can aid one in confirming a causal relationship which may be used to predict behaviors in the future (Johnson and Christensen, 2010). According to positivists, humans should possess rationality, objectivity and precision. This is why analysis, measurement and prediction approach tools are aided by a research philosophy.

The major pillars established in these research philosophies include positivism (reality), interprevitism realism and pragmatism. As slightly depicted, positivism is about what is real. The followers of interprevitism believe that people must understand the distinction between humans and their role as social actors. The believers of realism advocate that the existence of objects is not dependent on the knowledge of any given person or entity. Followers of pragmatism argue that people can embrace both interprevitism and positivism when understanding their surrounding world (Hatch and Cunliffe, 2006).

3.2.1 Positivism Philosophy

This study adopted the positivism philosophy which is founded on objectivity. Cooper and Schindler (2006) expound on this concept by stating that researchers who believe in this philosophy aim at obtaining results and making conclusions by being objective as opposed to being subjective. In this case, the researcher chooses data from a larger data sample and then bases his/her results/conclusion on the data sample collected independent of their beliefs or views on the research question at hand. This philosophy is highly used by researchers dealing with experimental and observational studies (Sagepub, 2014). Positivism is based on highly structured methods which are comprehensive when collecting quantifiable observations used to gain generalized results supported by statistical techniques.

3.2.2 Research Design

A descriptive research design determines and reports the way things are (Mugenda and Mugenda, 2003). The findings of Creswell (2003) observed that a descriptive research design is used when data is collected to describe persons, organizations, settings or phenomena. The causal relationship exist when changes in one variable causes change in the other. The descriptive survey design will be adopted and used to collect raw data, creating data structures and information that allow decision making or modeling cause-effect relationships between independent variables. Kothari (2008) in his study observed that the design also has enough provision for protection of bias and maximized reliability.

Descriptive design uses a preplanned design for analysis (Mugenda and Mugenda, 2003). Descriptive survey is a method of collecting information by interviewing or administering a questionnaire to a sample of individual (Orodho, 2003). Research design is a guideline of how one goes about answering the research questions that clearly defines purpose, and has consistency between the research questions and the proposed research method (Sekaran, 2010). Orodho (2003) in a study on research method overview contented that research design is an outline with procedures to provide answers to the research problem.

3.3 Target Population

Researchers define target population as a set of items that are to be included in the study. In this case the national government functions have been devolved into departments at county government. Nairobi County Government has a workforce of 6000 employees in eight departments according to the county government records as at Aug 2015. However, the total number of employees directly involved in financial and procurement related aspects total to 87 as detailed in table 1 below.

The study targeted the directors, senior managers, middle level managers, and support staff from the county of Nairobi who are directly related with financial aspects of the government. It was expected that employees working in finance and procurement department were the ideal respondents in order obtain the relevant insights that could help to answer the study questions.

According to NCG, the following is the number of employees in the county of Nairobi government.

TABLE 1

Sample Size of the Study

Category	Study Population	Sample Size	Sample
Directors and Deputies	16	100%	16
Senior Managers	16	100%	16
Middle Level Managers	16	100%	16
Support Staff	39	100%	39
Total Population	87	100%	87

Source (NCG 2015)

Sekaran (2005) observes that a research population is generally a large collection of common data from which samples are taken for analysis. It is for the benefit of the population that researches are done. However, due to the large sizes of populations, researchers often cannot test every individual in the population because it is too expensive and time-consuming. This study used 87 respondents in order to answer the study objectives efficiently and effectively. By targeting the directors and deputy directors, senior managers, middle level managers, and support staff – all from finance and procurement or dealing with financial aspects of the government, the study ensured that knowledgeable respondents were involved the data collection, to ensure that the study results are generalizable.

3.4 Sample Frame

A sample is the segment of the population that is selected for investigation. It is also a subgroup of the elements of the population selected for participation in the study (Bryman, 2012). This study uses the Krejcie and Morgan (1970) table of determining sample size from the population as shown in table1. It is observed that a sample frame is a listing of all elements in the population from which the sample is drawn. The purpose of sampling frames, which is to provide a means for choosing the particular members of the target population that are to be interviewed in the survey (Bennett, 1993).

In this study, the sampling unit is composed of the directors and deputies, senior managers, middle level managers, and support staff. This study used purposive sampling technique where all possible respondents are listed, no duplication of names contact of respondents provided, accurate to date and for the intended research. This method presents a challenge to the researcher when collecting data from the stakeholders due to varied expectations. The selection criteria were based on the number of procurement practitioners and managers in the supply chain. All the employees of the county government were included in the study, giving a total of 87respondents. According to

Cochran (1977) a sampling frame is a complete list of all the members of the population that we wish to study to randomly select an appropriate number as representatives of the population whom you can invite to take part in the research. Failure to use a sampling frame restricts to less satisfactory forms of samples which cannot be randomly selected because not all individuals within that population will have the same probability of being selected for the sample.

3.4.1 Sample size and sampling techniques

The purpose of sampling is to draw conclusion from a sample based on selected features and attributes that represents the whole population. The sampling strategy used in this study is nonprobability purposive sampling strategy which ensured that the key respondents participated in the study. In this study, a purposive sampling technique was adopted where all the 87 staff in eight departments – including directors and deputies, senior managers, middle level managers, and support staff, who were directly involved in either finance or procurement were issued with a self-administered questionnaire. The questionnaire comprised of both closed-ended and open ended questions.

Researchers observe three factors that influence sample representativeness; sample processing, size and participation response. Mugenda and Mugenda (2003) in a study on research methods, quantitative and qualitative approaches asserts that sampling is that part of the statistical practice concerned with the selection of observations to yield knowledge and possible statistical inferences. Sekaran (2005) in his finding on research methods for business, a skill building approach observes that the characteristics of a sample are a reflection the population from which it is drawn. According to Mugenda and Mugenda (2003), a researcher would have to use 30% of the total target population as a sample size for it to be accepted as a good representative sample. For the purpose of this study, all the respondents had sufficient knowledge on how procurement contract determinants could influence the organizational performance.

Yamane (1967) has a simplified formula for calculating sample size. At 95% confidence level as $P = .05$ especially for huge populations.

$$n=N/(1+N(e2)) \qquad n = 87/(1+87(0.1)^2)$$

$$= 87/(1+0.87)$$

$$46.524$$

$$\text{There sample size} = 47$$

Where: n= required response

e^2 = error limit

N = Sample size

Source: Yamane (1967:258)

3.5 Data Collection Instrument

The questionnaire was administered to the respondents using a drop and pick later method. The respondents were informed that the objective of the survey was to gather information about the procurement contract determinants: Internal Procurement Processes, Regulatory Framework, Leadership and Management Support and ICT Infrastructure Support. Respondents were assured that the information provided was confidential and purely for academic purpose only. The questionnaires were used as the primary source of data collection in eight departments. In this study 87 numbered questionnaires were distributed to the directors, senior managers, middle level managers and Support staff. Mugenda and Mugenda (2005) observe that questionnaires should be open and closed-ended in order to enable effective data collection. Primary data was preferred in this study because the data would be up to date and much more accurate since it was collected by the researcher himself for the purpose of the specific study. It differs from the secondary data which are the data obtained from the written materials which include journals, conference papers, research papers, magazines, books and other relevant materials. Sekaran (2005) pinpoints that secondary data enables the researcher to make comparison between the data obtained from the questionnaires with the written materials. The questionnaire was used since it was easy to administer and with data obtained easy to analyze (KIPPRA, 2005). The validity and reliability tests were carried out.

3.6 Validity and Reliability

The research instrument in the study was pre–tested to increase the validity of the responses (Blaikie, 2000). The purpose was to make sure that everyone in a sample not only understands the questions, but understands them in the same way (Bennett, 1993). The reason why the research instrument should be subjected to a pretest is to remove errors detected (Mugenda and Mugenda, 2003). Expert validity views and suggestions of the supervisors' were incorporated in the questionnaire and then pre-testing was done on 15 August 2015 with by administering 10 questionnaires to the researcher's 10 colleagues. These respondents were not included in the study sample. As a result of the pilot test, necessary changes in words selection and instructions were made to the questionnaire. To improve on accuracy, relevance, consistency, completeness, and uniformity of the data collected regular cross-checking and follow ups were implemented.

Reliability analysis was used to measure the consistency of the questionnaire. Reliability is defined as a measure of the degree to which a research instrument yields consistent results of collected data after repeated results (Mugenda and Mugenda, 2003). A Cronbach's alpha test of the instrument gave $\alpha=0.846$ which were interpreted as acceptable. It was observed that values of Cortina (2008) in a study on an examination of theory and applications established an alpha value threshold at 0.7 or 70% was regarded as most reliable. A Cronbach's α around 0.8 are good and the minimum acceptable limit is 0.5.

This was expressed using the following formulae.

$$\alpha = \frac{N.\bar{C}}{\bar{\bar{V}} + (N-1).\bar{C}}$$

Where:-

N- is the number of question items

$\bar{C}$- is the average inter-item covariance among items

$\bar{V}$- is the average variance

The test instrument is expected to be reliable to enable and the study to proceed for data collection.

3.7 Data Analysis and Presentation

Sekaram (2003) in his finding explains the three critical areas in data analysis as examining the data, subjecting the data to test, and answering the research question. Researchers observe that establishing subjecting the data to test lends credibility to all subsequent analysis and findings because it measures the reliability and the validity of the measures used in the study.

The gathered data from questionnaires was checked adequately for reliability and clarification. The data was entered into excel spread sheet. The data that was qualitative in nature was coded and organized into themes and organized accordingly. The researcher applied quantitative techniques to analyze the data and the findings were presented in the form of tables and figures for good understanding of the study findings and used to complete the study report.

The answers from the Likert scale ratings on extent of impact of procurement contract determinants: Internal Procurement Processes, Regulatory Framework, Leadership and Management Support and ICT Infrastructure Support on performance were collated and analyzed using Statistical Package for Social Sciences (SPSS Version 20). The analysis involved establishing the nature of the relationship between the variable and followed ordinary linear least square (OLS). Factor analysis was conducted on dependent and independent variable items and reliability analysis for the retained items was computed. The ANOVA table and coefficients results were interpreted and conclusions drawn as per the study objectives.

The relationship between the study variables can be expressed using the following multiple linear regression model;

Regression equation: $Y = \beta_0 + \beta_1 X_1 + \beta_2 X_2 + \beta_3 X_3 + \beta_4 X_4 + \varepsilon$, where

β_0 is regression intercept; β_1-β_4 are the regression coefficients and Y is the dependent variable (Organizational performance), X_1= internal procurement processes is independent variable, X_2 = Leadership and Management support is independent variable, X_3=policy regulatory frame work is independent variable and X_4= ICT infrastructure support is independent variable. The results were presented in the form of frequency tables, pie charts and bar graphs.

$$Y = \beta_0 + \beta_1 X_1 + \beta_2 X_2 + \beta_3 X_3 + \beta_4 X_4 + \varepsilon, \text{ where}$$

Y= Dependent variable (Organizational performance)

X_1=Independent variable (Internal Procurement Processes)

X_2= Independent variable (Policy Regulatory Framework)

X_3= Independent variable (Leadership and Management Support)

X_4= Independent variable (ICT Infrastructure Support)

$\beta 1 - \beta 4$ = Regression coefficient for each independent variable

ε −Random or stochastic term

3.8 Pilot Test Results

Before actual data collection a pilot study was carried out on 10 respondents to determine reliability of the questionnaires to be administered. The pilot study involved sampling respondents of the target group in the organizations. Reliability analysis using Cronbach's Alpha was used to measure the internal consistency of the collected data.

A study undertaken by Cortina (2008) on Cronbach alpha established the threshold value of Alpha at 0.7 or better was regarded accurate and reliable. Forming the study's Cronbach Alpha threshold was set as the study's benchmark and thus established for every objective which formed a scale. The table below shows that Leadership and Management Support had the highest reliability (α=0.815), followed by policy regulatory framework (α=0.813), Internal Procurement Processes (α=0.811) and ICT Infrastructure Support (α=0.810). All the four variables were reliable with Alpha threshold more than 0.7. Table 2 below shows the results.

TABLE 2

Pilot test results

Scale	Cronbach's Alpha	Number of Items
Internal Procurement Processes	0.811	5
Policy Regulatory Framework	0.813	5
Leadership and Management Support	0.815	5
ICT Infrastructure Support	0.810	5

CHAPTER FOUR

FINDINGS AND DISCUSSION

4.1 Introduction

The chapter provides the results and interpretation and discussion of the findings obtained from the field. The background information of the respondents and findings from the analysis based on the objectives of the study is also provided. The findings are organized in tables and figures. The discussions are done immediately after interpretation of each finding. The ensuing section consists of the background information of the respondents.

4.2 Background Information

The overall objective of this study was to investigate the effect of public procurement contract determinants such as: Internal Procurement Processes, Regulatory Framework, Leadership and Management Support and ICT Infrastructure Support on organizational performance. The study followed descriptive study design. The researcher conducted purposive sampling of the 87 respondents including directors and deputies, senior managers, middle level managers, and support officers the Nairobi county government using semi-structured questionnaires. The researcher managed to obtain 81 completed questionnaires whose information was used to complete this report. This represents 93.10 percent which is appropriate return rate to make generalizable conclusions going by conclusions of Baruch (1999) who concludes that 55 percent is sufficient return rate for social science studies.

4.2.1 Gender of the Respondents

The researcher sought information regarding the gender of the respondents. The findings were as shown in table 3. The study results revealed that 59.3% of the respondents were male while 40.7% were female. This revealed that the respondents of both gender were involved to enrich the study results.

TABLE 3

Gender of the Respondents

Gender of the respondent	Tally	Percentage
Male	48	59.3%
Female	33	40.7%
Total	**81**	**100%**

Notably, female and male respondents may view a situation in an organization differently simply due to their orientation. To this end, gender balance in any research undertaking is essential to ensure that variations related to gender are captured into the study (Eriksson and Kovalainen, 2008). By including respondents of diverse gender high quality research findings were obtained.

Also, the respondents were asked to indicate their work experience. The results were as shown in table 4. The study findings revealed that 27%, 47%, 23% and 3% were in experience brackets; less than 2 years, 2-6 years, 7-10 years and above 10 years respectively. Notably, apart from the 27% who had experience of less than 2 years, majority of the respondents had experience of more than 2 years. This means that the respondents had reasonable experience to give reliable insights that could enrich the results of the study and arrive at generalizable conclusions.

TABLE 4

Work Experience

Work Experience	Tally	Percentage
Less than 2 years	22	27%
2-6 years	38	47%
7-10 years	19	23%
Above 10 years	2	3%
Total	**81**	**100%**

By involving respondents with reasonable work experience, the study conclusions are based on opinions of respondents with experience in the field of study. Mugenda (2003) notes that experience of the respondents enriches the study conclusions since it increases the quality of the study findings.

Further, the researcher obtained the level of education of the targeted respondents and establish and the results were as shown in table 5. The study results show that 20%, 40%, 23.3% and 16.7% of the respondents had master degree, bachelor degree, diploma, and certificate respectively. This shows that all the respondents had requisite education level to read and comprehend the questionnaire and give relevant answer.

TABLE 5

Level of Education of the Respondents

Level of Education	Tally	Percentage
Masters	16	20.0%
Bachelors	32	40.0%
Diploma	19	23.3%
Certificate	14	16.7%
Total	**81**	**100.0%**

The level of education of the respondent is associated with the quality of the study results. Mugenda (2003) posits that the target respondent should have relevance understanding of the area of the study. The level of education enriches an individual and broadens their thinking ability. This coupled with the reasonable experience as earlier noted and the fact that the respondents were given ample time to complete the questionnaire as well as the opportunity to ask where they need clarification are essential ingredients to ensure that the relevant insights were obtained from the respondents.

4.3 Effect of Internal Procurement Processes on Performance

The researcher sought to establish the effect of internal procurement processes on organization performance. In this regard, the respondents were asked to rate the nature of procurement processes in their organization in relation to performance as described by the statements shown in table 6. The study results showed that the respondents agreed with the statement that their organization has articulate internal procurement processes.

They also agreed with the view that internal control processes are responsible for and do positively influence the performance in their organization. However, they were neutral (indifferent) whether the employees do relate internal procurement processes with performance. In light of the findings, it can be concluded that the respondents trust the robustness of their organization's procurement procedures but the employees do mistakenly dissociate the procurement control processes with their performance and do not follow the procedures and policy and regulations as would be expected.

TABLE 6

Relationship between Internal Procurement Processes and Performance

Internal Procurement Procedures and Performance	Average rating	Conclusion
My company has articulate Internal Procurement Processes	2.50	Agree
The Internal Procurement Processes are responsible for Organizational Performance	2.00	Agree
Employees do not relate Internal Procurement Processes with their Performance	3.17	Neutral
The presence of Internal Procurement Processes do positively influence Organizational Performance	1.93	Agree

This findings was consistent with the conclusions of PPDA (2010) who observed that Procurement contract implementation in public institutions been viewed negatively due perceived inefficiency, corruption and disregard of pursuit of value addition in the organizations. More often than not, the junior officers flaw the procurement processes and disregard policy with minimal or no questioning by their senior officers who do not follow the laid down regulations in their actions. According to Tan *et al.* (2009), this incorrect dissociation does adversely impact the rate and quality of progress in realizing the objectives of county development.

Also, the respondents were asked to state the role of the procurement processes in an organization. The findings were as shown in figure 5 below. The study results indicated above shows that 28.6%, 24.7%, 17.3%, 12.3%, 9.9% and 7.4% of the respondents said that procurement processes do enhance purchase quality, enhances controls in the organization, manages possible self-interests, increases efficiency and effectiveness, supports organizational goals, and ensure that all departments are appropriately equipped. In this view, procurement

70

processes are essential in ensuring order in the purchases function of an organization which would in turn increase organizational performance.

The key finding was that internal procurement processes do enhance purchase quality, enhances controls in the organization, and manages possible self-interests (corruption), as well as increase efficiency and effectiveness. To this end, organizations with robust procurement processes can attain better performance if the processes are articulately followed. This is essential because procurement department is responsible for sourcing and obtaining the required goods and services which involves exchange of value and affects the organization.

FIGURE 5

The role of Internal Procurement Processes on Performance

The findings concurs with the revelations of Salem (2003) who argued that management in contracting authorities should ensure that good practice in purchasing is backed by appropriate procedures to ensure compliance with all relevant guidelines. Also, Drucker (2011) believes that process improvements transform business and lead to innovation and represent "the change that creates a new dimension of performance" for organizations. Therefore the process should be improved from period to period to ensure better results for the procurement function and entire organization.

In addition, the respondents were asked to rate the extent to which procurement processes does influence the performance of their organization. The study shown in figure 6 below indicate that 50% of the respondents rated to a very great extent that internal procurement processes do influence performance. Also, 36.7% of the respondents rated to great extent while 13.3% were neutral as regarding the relationship between internal procurement processes on performance.

Notably, majority of the respondents (86.7%) do believe that internal procurement processes are important as they indicated that it does influence the overall performance of their organization. The respondents explained that the procurement processes in their organization influenced the performance of their organization because it determines the quality of the acquired service or good. It also ensures that efficiency is attained in the organization – that the organization does not lose money where it could be avoided by acquiring quality goods at a cheaper cost. The key aim in regard to this finding is ensuring that value for money is responsibly enhanced with shareholder and key stakeholder being kept in mind (Porter, 1985.

Extent to which Internal Procurement Processes Influences Performance

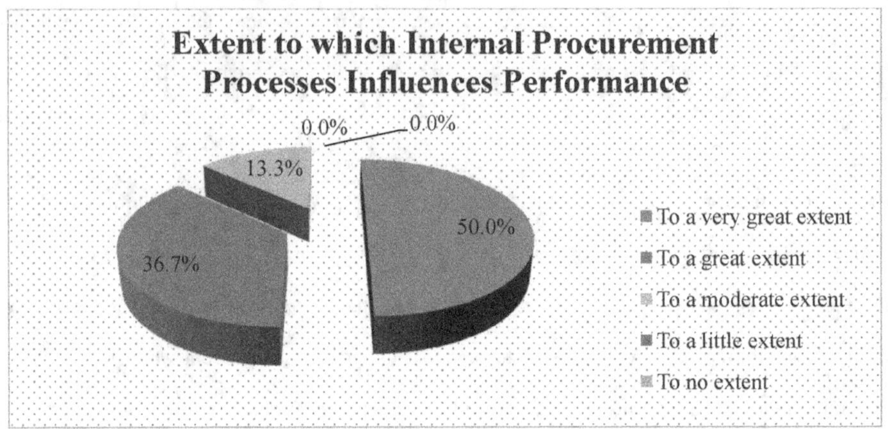

The finding was congruent with the views of Muhochi et al. (2010) on opportunities and challenges of Business Process Management (BPM) as he concludes that effective implementation and control of internal procurement processes does enhance organization financial outcomes. Drucker (2011) agrees with this view and points out that BPM do empower companies to align internal procurement processes to provide more value to both internal and external customers. In his conclusion Smith and Conway (1993) identified seven essential success factors which influence procurement, including a clear procurement strategy, effective management information and control systems, and communication of the key success factors to diverse levels of the organization.

To establish how the internal procurement processes do influence organizational performance, the respondents were requested to state exactly how they felt these processes did influence the performance of their organization. The findings were as shown in figure 7 below. The results show that 34%, 24%, 17%, 14% and 10% of the respondents felt that the internal procurement processed; helps the organization to avoid duplication of roles, helps attain timely and accurate deliverable of inputs, helps the business to plan ahead, makes things clear and boosts integration, as well as create friendly environment in that order. To this end, articulate procurement processes are essential in an organization as it has several positive attributes, at least as revealed by the study.

How Internal Procurement Processes influences Performance

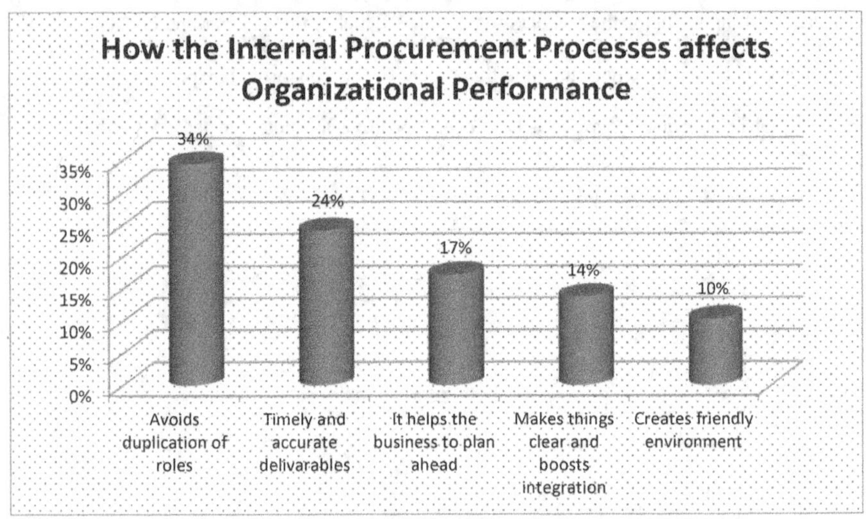

The key findings were that internal procurement processes do influence organization performance because it helps avoid duplication of roles, ensures timely and accurate purchases and helps the organization to plan ahead. To this end, if the entity officers would follow the procurement processes to the latter, the inherent malpractices evidenced in most procurement functions would be minimized and eventually eradicated (Posner, 1993). This is true at least as per the conclusions of Callender and Schapper (2003) who assert that realization of procurement goals is influenced by internal and external forces. According to World Bank (2007) while studying local government budgeting process argues that budget process and execution of the same should be incorporated into managerial decision making process through management information system to help attain effective budgetary reporting. This can help defeat the tendency of officers to defraud the organization by following their own designed processes for personal gain.

4.4 Effect of Policy and Regulatory Framework on Performance

Another aim of this study was to establish the effect of policy and regulation framework on organizational performance. Firstly, the respondents were asked to state the importance of policy in their organization. The findings were as shown in figure 8 below. The results in figure 4.4 indicate that 33%, 26%, 19%, 17% and 5% of the respondents stated that policy and regulations; sets the specific parameters under which to operate, helps to avoid a one man opinion, ensures adherence to ethical conduct, promotes competition and innovation as well as enhance value and quality respectively. The major findings included that policy and regulatory frameworks sets specific parameters under which to operate, so as to avoid one man opinion. This ensures adherence to ethical conduct and enhances quality of purchases and attains value for the shareholders.

Importance of Policy and Regulatory Framework in an Organization

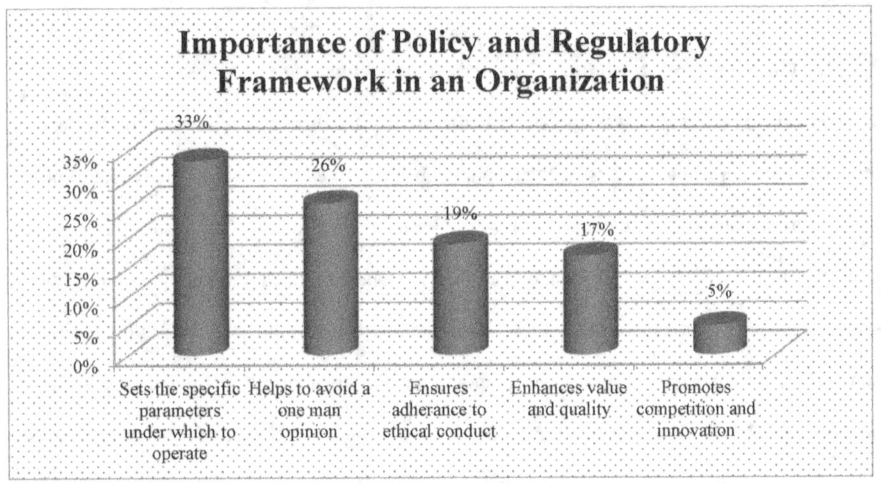

Notably, the existence of appropriate policy is in itself essential. The study noted that adherence to the set regulations and compliance to policy is critical for organizational performance. While the aforementioned roles of policy and regulatory framework are ingredients for better performance, it is conformity by the officers involved in the procurement process that ensures maximum value creation for the company. The conclusion agrees with Minahan (2007) who posits that that it is essential to design public contracts that are robust within government policy regulatory framework to enhance organizational performance. Spiller (2008) adds that compliance with applicable regulatory and policies can enhance procurement practice quality.

Also, the respondents were asked to rate the extent to which they felt that independent policy and regulatory framework in their organization did influence performance. The results were as shown in figure 9. The findings indicate that 66.7% of the respondents felt that policy and regulatory framework does influence performance to a very great extent. Also, 30% said that policy and framework influences performance to a great extent while only 3.3% were neutral. To this end, majority of the respondents said that regulatory framework influences organizational performance.

FIGURE 9

Extent to which Policy and Regulatory Framework Influences Performance

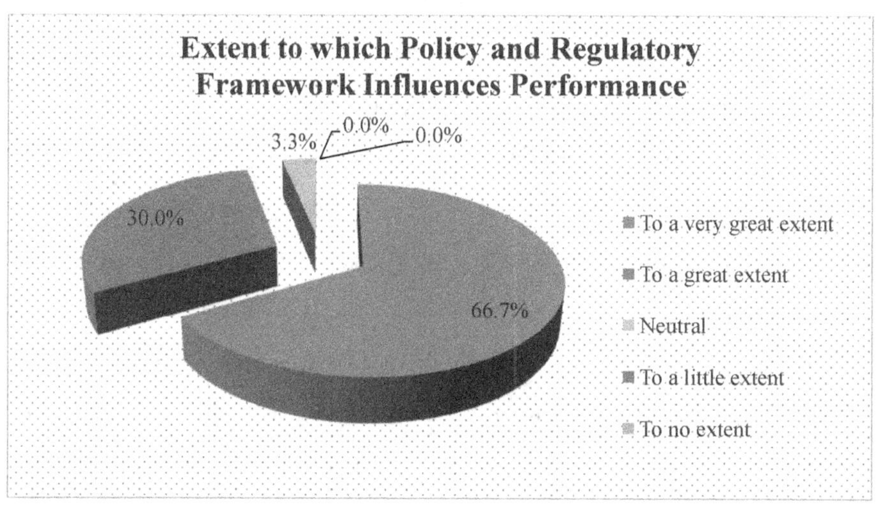

The finding supports the suppositions by McIvor (2000) who posited that policy broadly guides the actions of the employees in an organization while regulations guide the intricate decisions of the officers as they execute each and every procurement contract (Porter, 1985). The study concurs with conclusions of Spiller (2008) who argues that compliance with applicable obligations can enhance procurement practice. In this view, the regulations should already be in existence for them to be adhered unto. Also, Apiyo and Mburu (2014) on factors affecting procurement planning in county governments in Kenya concluded that creating a functional management or regulatory body and strengthening the institution's capacity can positively influence performance.

Also, the respondents were asked to explain why they thought policy and framework do influence their organizational performance. The results were as shown in figure 10 below. The findings in figure 4.6 above shows that 34.6%, 27.2%, 18.5%, 11.1% and 8.6% of the respondents explained that policy and regulatory framework influences organizational performance because it creates a level playing field, shapes the environment for decision making, acts as a guide for the employees, upholds standards of quality as well as enhance monitoring the processes respectively. Also, policy and regulations within organizations helps the employees to act within specified bounds and creates value for the company. Officers of a company should rely on the policy and regulations in all decisions they make. Unless the officers act in line with policy and regulations, quality can be compromised and value for money disregarded (Posner, 1993). When it comes to adherence to policy and regulations of an organization, all employees should comply led by their seniors (Sanders, et al., 2007). All procurement decisions should be based on the requirements of the policy and regulations of the organization to ensure value for money (Sharma and Jain, 2013).

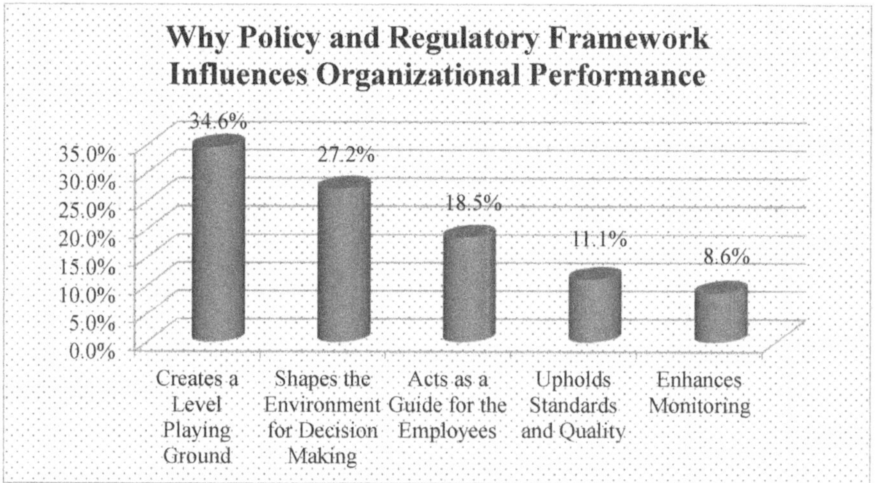

These revelations concurs with Arthur (2009) who pointed out that putting in place an efficient and effective contract administration mechanism is essential for the national and county governments performance. Ongore and K'Obonyo (2011) add that introducing ethics and anticorruption measures in public procurement regulations is essential because employees need to have appropriate bounds of practice. Also, Callender and Schapper (2003) held that reform to safeguard the integrity of the procurement system by establishing and increasing control and audit system are essential for performance.

4.5 Effect of Leadership and Management Support on Organizational Performance

Also, the study sought to establish the effect of leadership Support on opportunity performance. The respondents were asked to state the importance of leadership and management support of procurement endeavors in an organization. The summarized findings were as shown in figure 11. The study results revealed that 40.7%, 27.2%, 18.5% and 13.6% of the respondents vouched that leadership support to procurement endeavors in an organization is important because leaders have the responsibility to encourage and guide the employees, they understand the processes much better, they are the key decision making organ and because it boosts the potential of other departments respectively.

Notably, everything falls and rises with the leadership. The leaders and managers must be at the forefront in as far as obedience to the policy and regulatory frameworks of an organization; they must lead for their junior officers to follow (Williamson, 2002). Furthermore, the leaders and managers must be capable to lead their team into doing right (Wymer and Regan, 2005).

Importance of Leadership Support on Organizational Performance

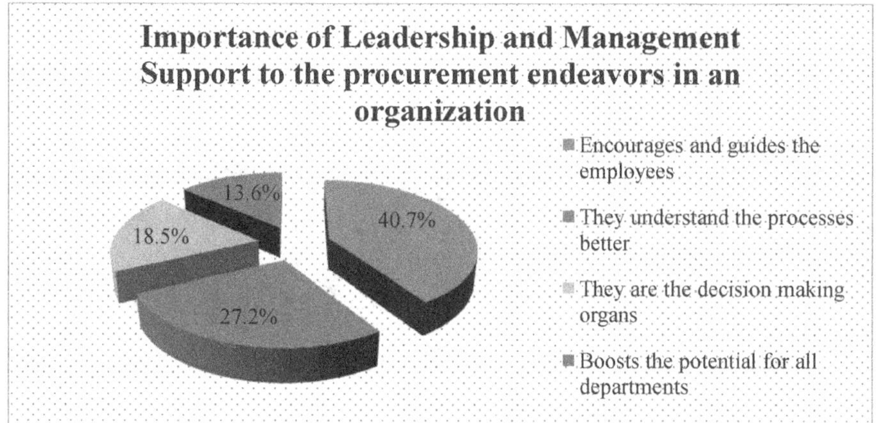

In light of the findings organization leaders and managers; must know and be seen doing what is right, do what is right, instruct their juniors to do what is right, and be accountable for the mistakes that occur in their departments. The finding concurs with the conclusions of Abbas and Asghar (2010) who concluded that leaders are the ones who have the vision of what can be achieved and then communicate this to their junior colleagues as well as evolve the strategies for realizing the vision. It also rhymes with the views of Were *et al.* (2012) who noted that they motivate people and are able to negotiate for resources and other support to achieve their goals. Also, Abbas and Asghar (2010) concluded that a manager must also be a leader to achieve optimum results.

In investigating the effect of leadership and management support to procurement functions on organizational performance, the respondents were asked to rate the extent to which they felt that leadership and management support did affect the performance of their organization. The findings were as summarized in figure 12. The study results revealed that 59%, 35% and 6% of the respondents were of the opinion that leadership support affects organizational performance to a very great extent, to a great extent and neutral respectively. Notably, majority of the respondents (94%) felt that leadership support to procurement endeavors does influence performance in an organization. This reveals that leaders are the ones to steer the company to the great heights by being good examples to their junior employees in deeds and words (Steinberg, 2003).

FIGURE 12

Extent to which Leadership Support Influences Performance

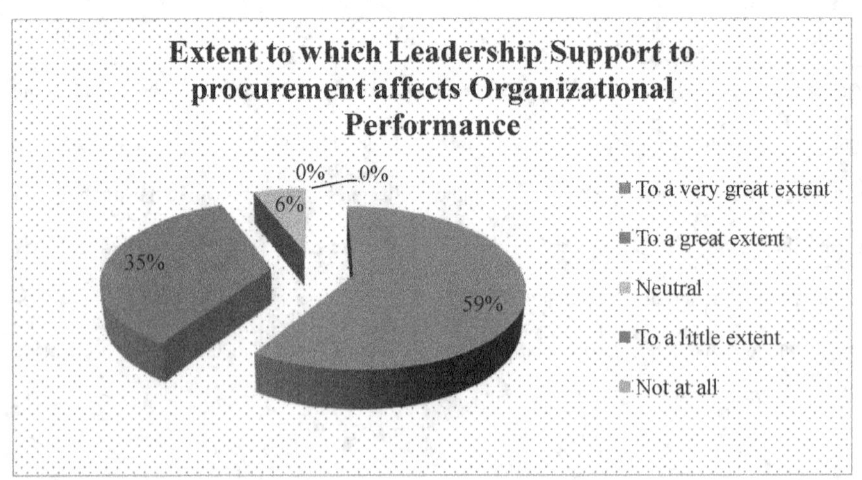

The finding is congruent to conclusions of Rashid and Al-Qirim (2001) who established that leadership and management support is critical for successful implementation of e-procurement and strategies that can support success of the business. According to Mamiro (2010), lack of proper internal procurement processes, leadership and management structure, unrealistic budgets and inadequacy of skills of procurement practitioners are the major challenges in public procurement. No doubt, these limitations do hinder performance. Furthermore, Kakwezi and Nyeko (2010) concluded that failure to establish performance of the procurement function for public entities can lead to inefficient, irregular and costly consequences to the organizational performance. To this end, management support is essential to organization performance.

In investigating the contribution of leadership support on procurement and performance of the organization, the respondents were asked to explain why leadership support does influence performance of an organization's procurement function. The study results summarized in figure 13 below shows that 33.3%, 24.7%, 22.2%, 11.1% and 8.6% of the respondents felt that the procurement leadership/management does influence performance in their organization because they are the custodians of morals in an organization, they provide direction to the organization, they encourage and support the staffs, guides the junior officers to what is expected and are the main decision makers in an organization respectively. Notably, the respondents considered their leaders and managers as the key ingredients fin regards morals in the organization and for organization success.

Why Leadership Support influences Performance

The finding is consistent with the revelations of Abbas and Asghar (2010) who established that a significant relationship between organizational change and leadership characterized with vision and innovation. This means that if the management does not do their part to a certain threshold, success is not guaranteed because junior officers only take after their management. However, leadership involvement and close look of the procurement endeavors is minimal in most organizations. For instance a survey on CEOs perspectives on supply chain management by Eisenstein and Thompson (2006) revealed that most CEOs were responsible for driving development and execution of contracts as this is delegated to junior officers.

4.6 Extent of the ICT Infrastructure on Organizational Performance

In addition, the researcher investigated the effect of ICT infrastructure on organizational performance. In this pursuit, the respondents were asked to rate the extent of the robustness of the ICT Infrastructure in their organization. The findings were as shown in figure 14. Amongst the target sampled respondents, the study established that that 39%, 30% and 25% of the respondents rated the robustness of the ICT infrastructure in their organization; to a great extent, moderate extent, and very great extent respectively while 6% felt it is not adequate. While the respondents said that they have got appropriate ICT infrastructure, the need for supporting such structures is essential.

FIGURE 14

Extent to which ICT Infrastructure support Influences Performance

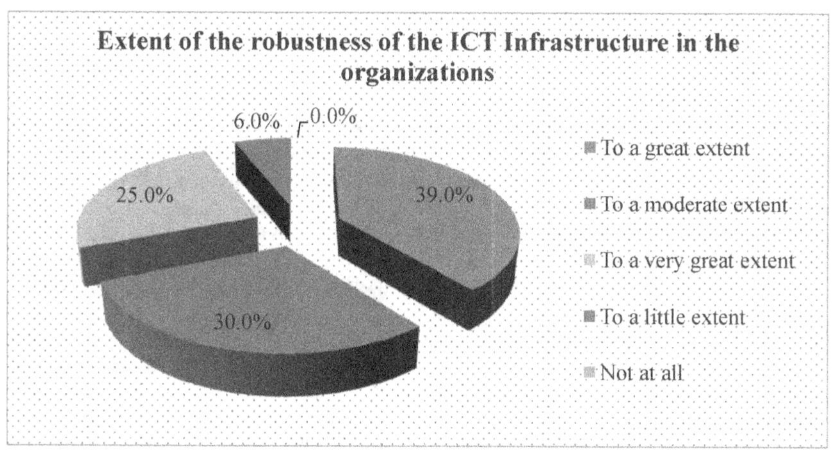

The study results shown above reveal that majority of the respondents rated that robust ICT infrastructure do influence performance, at least to a great extent. In particular, supporting the ICT infrastructure is essential. Mere presence of the required technology and tools cannot amount to success of the organization. This support should originate from the management and leadership who act as the cheer leaders to their junior staffs for holistic organizational success. To this end, ICT do influence organizational performance. This agrees with Liker and Choi (2004) and Kazimoto (2013) who noted that ICT influences performance since it eases communications and understanding with suppliers as well as increases service quality and employee output. This is consistent with revelations of Van Weel (2006) who noted that adoption and use of ICT has increased over time since there has been a surge in suppliers enabled supply chain in most sectors. Courtesy to ICT adoption Minihan (2007) noted that users have fewer motives to try to outwit the system.

Also, the respondents were asked to explain how ICT infrastructure influences organizational performance. The findings were as shown in figure 14. The findings show that 31%, 22%, 19%, 16% and 13% of the respondents explained that ICT; enhances efficiency, enhances monitoring and control, makes work easy, enhances communication and makes service delivery easier in that order. Notably, ICT infrastructure has got several advantages in an organization. However, it has to be supported by all the participants. Otherwise, some members of the organization may continue with paper work or they may still indulge in behaviors that still affect the organization negatively (Wenyang, 2005). Kramer et al (2007), notes that leaders should be at the forefront when it comes to encouraging their staffs to use a particular technology.

How ICT Infrastructure Influences the Organizational Performance

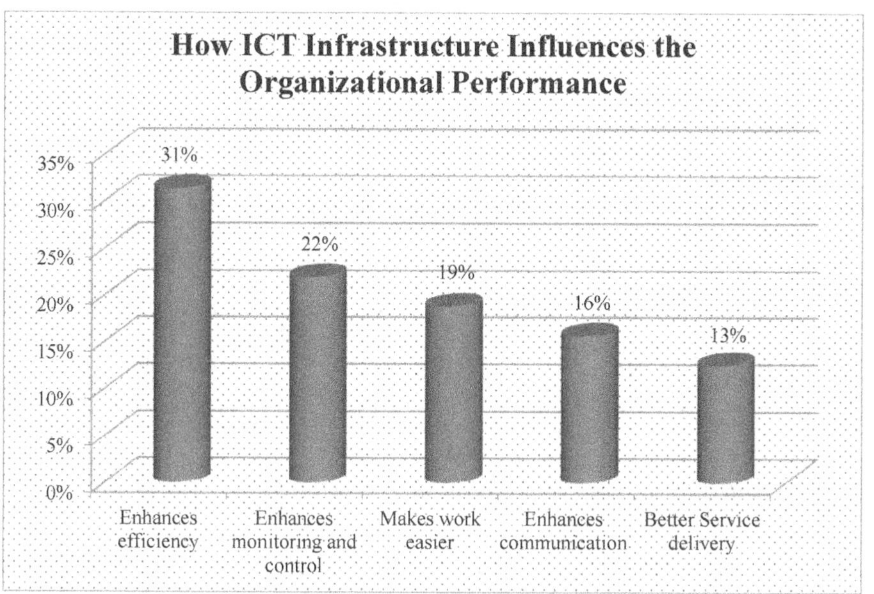

The aspects mentioned to have been realized due to ICT are associated with entity performance by Kramer et al. (2007). Also, Ellram (1995) factors resulting from implementation of ICT as follows; two-way information sharing, top management support, shared goals, early communication to suppliers and supplier adds distinctive value. However, Orina (2013) identified finance, leadership, legal framework and staff competence as key factors in implementing e-procurement in the public sector. Oketch (2014) concluded that lack of experienced personnel as hindrance for seamless transition from manual to electronic procurement environment in most organizations.

4.7 Regression Analysis

In investigating the relationship between the study variables, the respondents were asked to rate in a Likert scale of 1-10 (where 1 meant poor and 10 excellent) the extent to which they viewed the public procurement contract determinants; Internal Procurement Processes, Regulatory Framework, Leadership and Management Support and ICT Infrastructure as being effective in their organization. They also rated the extent to which these variables did influence performance in their organization. To measure performance, the respondents rated in a Likert scale of 1-10, the extent to which the procurement contract determinants above had influenced the four elements of performance (Financial, Customer Service, Internal Organizational Processes, and Learning and Development) used to measure performance as per the BCG model developed by Kaplan and Norton (1992).

4.7.1 Test for Assumptions of Regression - Diagnostic Test

Before regression analysis was done, the researcher tested assumptions such as normality and multi collinearity.

Test for Normality

The researcher conducted the test for normality. This was done using the normal probability plot, which was also used to test for heteroscedasiticity. Figure 16 shows the test. For normally distributed data the mean, mode and median are very close to being equal. The normal probability graph revealed data sets that appear visually to be normally distributed in the process capability plot as shown in figure 16 below.

Normality Test

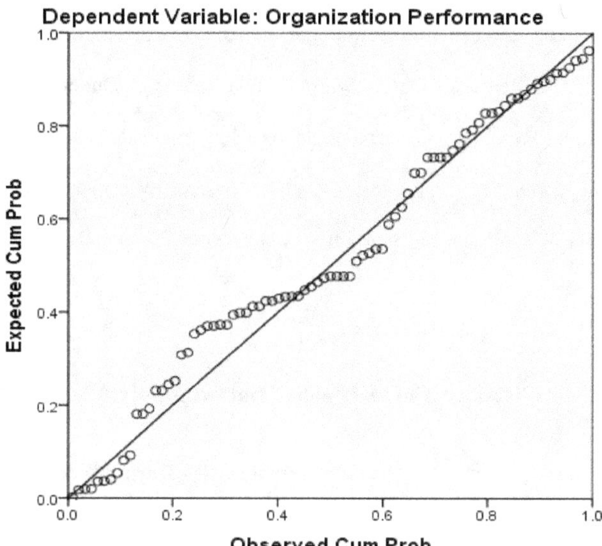

Test for Heteroscedasticity

It is defined as the variability of a variable being unequal across the range of values of a second variable that predicts it (Asteriou & Hall, 2011). It occurs when a scatter of residual errors varies differently with change of value of one or more predictor variables – the error term is said to be heteroskedastic. The scatter diagram above show that the model is generally linear with data sets around the linear line, hence there is no heteroscedasticity.

Test for Autocorrelation

This is also called serial correlation or cross-autocorrelation. It is the cross-correlation of a signal with itself at different points in time. Simply, it is the similarity between observations as a function of the time lag between them. Statisticians state that even in the presence of autocorrelation, the regression results still remain unbiased (Priestley, 1982). In this study, autocorrelation was Tested using Durbin Watson (DW) statistic. A Durbin Watson DW statistic around 2.0 shows lack of first order autocorrelation while a statistic equal to 4.0 shows lack of second order autocorrelation. The obtained Durbin Watson DW statistic was 1.725 as shown below. A Durbin Watson statistic near 2.0 reveals that there is no evidence of first-order autocorrelation.

TABLE 7

Test for Autocorrelation - Durbin Watson DW

Test	Test statistic - Durbin Watson DW
Auto-correlation	1.725

After ascertaining the assumptions of regression, the researcher conducted a regression. Independent variables public procurement contract determinants; Internal Procurement Processes, Regulatory Framework, Leadership and Management Support and ICT Infrastructure were regressed against performance in their organization using SPSS version 20. The analysis sought to determine the coefficients for the multiple regression model and the inferential statistics; the Pearson Product Moment/correlation coefficient R Square and the coefficient of determination R of the data set. The summaries of the regression results were as shown in the ensuing part of this report.

4.7.2 Model Summary Statistics

In order to establish the relationship between the study variables, the researcher used regression analysis to establish coefficient of determination (R) and correlation coefficient (R-Square). Coefficient of determination (R) measures the direction of the relationship while correlation coefficient measures the strength of the relationship. The findings were as shown in table 4.6. The study established coefficient of determination (R) of 0.867 and correlation coefficient (R-Square) of 0.752 while the adjusted R- Square was 0.726. Since R was large and positive, the results indicated a positive relationship between the study variables. With R Square being 0.752, the regression results indicated that there is a strong relationship between public contract determinants and organizational performance.

TABLE 8

Model Summary Statistics

Model	R	R Square	Adjusted R Square	Durbin-Watson
1	.867[a]	0.752	.726	1.725
a. Predictors: (Constant), ICT Infrastructure Support, Internal Procurement Processes, Policy Regulatory Framework, Leadership and management Support b. Dependent Variable: Organization Performance				

The results show that a large percentage of the change in organizational performance can be attributed to procurement contract determinants ICT Infrastructure Support, Internal Procurement Processes, Policy Regulatory Framework, Leadership and management Support. Consequently, an improvement to these variables can alter organization performance positively. In this regard, organizational leaders can alter organizational performance positively by improving the aspects that influence success of a company (Van Weele, 2006). Victor (2012) said that enhancing procurement quality saves the money for the shareholders and ensures that the company has got the right inputs for better performance.

Lee (2007) carrying a study on impacts of organization resources on agency performance and described resources in terms of qualified staff, budgets, enabling environment, information technology, specific intellectual property and others. Lee (2007) pointed out that sourcing the right mix of inputs helps an organization to attain the success. For this to happen, Kazimoto (2013) observed that the actions of the officers, through the support of the leadership should be well intended for the organization. This is essential because leadership involves defining and communicating an organization's long-term vision and mission. They use their influence to improve the organization as well as manage possible conflicts and shape the change needed by the organization that they manage (Porter, 1985).

4.7.3 Analysis of Variance

The analysis also involved analysis of variance in order to test the statistical significance of the model. In testing the statistical significant of the regressions results of the analysis, probability-statistic (p-value) and F-test statistic was used. Regressions results with a p-value less that 0.05 are usually deemed as statistically significant meaning that the results can be relied upon to draw conclusions. The findings were as shown in table 4.6 below.

TABLE 9

Analysis of Variance

Model	Sum of Squares	Df	Mean Square	F	Sig.
Regression	17.988	4	4.497	5.569	.001[b]
Residual	61.370	76	807		
Total	79.358	80			
a. Dependent Variable: Organization Performance					
b. Predictors: (Constant), ICT Infrastructure Support, Internal Procurement Processes, Policy Regulatory Framework, Leadership Support					

From the ANOVA result's table above, a p-value of 0.001 was obtained implying that the regression obtained statistically significant results in predicting the relationship between the public procurement contract determinants and organization performance since the obtained p-value $(0.001<\alpha=0.05)$. Also, the F-test statistic obtained through the analysis is 5.569 which is less than the F-test tabulation at F80; 4; 0.05 which is equal to 5.69 which agree with P-value, in indicating that the regression results were statistically significant.

Successful and efficient procurement contract management practices are those that meet the needs of the company's stakeholders. They ensure that rational and efficient sourcing and application of funds; allows competition and manage the potential liabilities to the buyer. Arthur (2009) points out that enforcement of the public procurement requires efficient and effective contract administration and dispute resolution reforms, whether in the context of the national and county governments (PPDA, 2010). Callender and Schapper (2003) adds that other reforms include safeguarding the integrity of the procurement system by establishing and enhancing control and audit system. Such an environment can help to ensure that public procurement contract ingredients do influence performance. The environment requires application of information technology, adherence to processes and regulations guiding implementation of procurement function, but has to be supported by the senior officers in the organization (Hawthorne, 2013).

4.7.4 Regression Model Coefficients

Also, the regression analysis sought to establish the model coefficients. Model coefficients do reveal more information regarding the nature of the relationship between study variables (Lardenoije, et al., 2005). Table 4.7 below shows the model coefficients.

TABLE 10

Research Coefficients

Model	Unstandardized Coefficients	Standardized Coefficients	Sig.
	B	Beta	
(Constant)	5.536		.000
Internal Procurement Processes (x_1)	.200	341	.002
Policy Regulatory Framework (x_2)	.020	.029	.008
Leadership and Management Support (x_3)	.089	.123	.003
ICT Infrastructure Support (x_4)	.121	.182	.001
a. Dependent Variable: Organization Performance			

The analysis was undertaken at 5% confident level. The criteria for comparing whether the predictor variables were significant in the model was through comparing the corresponding probability value obtained and $\alpha=0.05$. If the probability value was less than α then the predictor variable was significant; otherwise it was not. Therefore, (Constant variable) and the Internal Procurement Processes were significant while Policy/Regulatory Framework, Leadership Support, ICT Infrastructure Support were individually insignificant as depicted by respective P-values equal to 0.000, 0.002, 0.008, 0.003 and 0.001 respectively. Furthermore, the obtained relationship is strong and positive as indicated by model summary statistics R and R-Square shown in table 4.7.

The obtained standardized coefficients were; 0.341, 0.029, 0.123 and 0.182 corresponding to Internal Procurement Processes, Leadership and management Support, Policy and Regulatory Framework and ICT Infrastructure Support respectively. Since the coefficients were positive, the model depicts a positive relationship. Therefore, a unit improvement on the four procurement contract determinants enhances performance by 0.341, 0.029, 0.123 and 0.182 corresponding to each of the variables, Internal Procurement Processes, Leadership and management Support, Policy and Regulatory Framework and ICT Infrastructure Support respectively. The multiple regression model describing the relationship between the study variables above can be expressed by the formula below;

$$Y = 5.536 + 0.341x_1 + 0.029x_2 + 0.123x_3 + 0.183x_4$$

The regression results as depicted by the model above indicate that there is a positive relationship between; Internal Procurement Processes, Leadership and management Support, Policy and Regulatory Framework and ICT Infrastructure Support with organizational performance. Also, the intercept – 5.536 was positive. It represents other factors that influence organizational performance. Therefore, managers should always endeavor to enhance these variables for in order to improve the performance in the organization. Therefore, organizations should enhance their procurement contract life cycle and ensure value for their organization. According to Porter (1985) contract life cycle management is the process of efficiently managing the contract creation, execution and analysis of the process with an aim to maximizing operational and financial performance and minimizing risks. The ultimate goal of public procurement is to provide the required goods and services in time within set budgets (Errigde and Mcllroy, 2002). This ought to be complimented by effective contract management geared towards high organizational performance. Public entities should overcome existing challenges in order to enhance procurement processes that make a saving and avoid wastage. Ntayi (2009) in his study observes that millions of dollars get wasted in many countries due to inefficient and ineffective obstacles and challenges in the procurement process of which contract management is a part.

CHAPTER FIVE

CONCLUSIONS AND RECOMMENDATIONS

5.1 Introduction

This chapter provides the summary of the study. It also provides the conclusions and recommendations of the study in light of the study objectives.

5.2 Summary of the study

The overall aim of this study was to investigate the effect of public procurement contract determinants such as: Internal Procurement Processes, Regulatory Framework, Leadership and Management Support and ICT Infrastructure Support on organizational performance. The study followed descriptive study design. The study was guided by the following study objectives; to determine the effect of internal procurement processes on organizational performance, to assess the effect of policy/regulatory framework on organizational performance, to investigate the effect of leadership and management support on organizational performance, and to investigate the effect of ICT infrastructure support on organizational performance.

The study followed a descriptive research design targeting the Nairobi County officials. With aid of 10 researcher assistants, the researcher targeted 87 finance and procurement departments officers in the Nairobi county government using semi-structured questionnaires. A drop and pick later technique was employed. The researcher managed to obtain 81 completed questionnaires (93.10 percent response rate) whose information was used to complete this report. Also, the respondents rated (in a Likert scale of 1-10) the extent to which they were satisfied by the status of   Internal Procurement Processes, Regulatory Framework, Leadership and Management

Support and ICT Infrastructure Support, as well as (extent to which the variables did) influence performance in their organization. The data was organized in excel spread sheets and analyzed using excel and SPSS version 20.

Regarding the effect of internal procurement processes on organizational performance, the sampled respondents stated that internal procurement processes do influence organizational performance. In relation to this, 6.1%, 9.8%, 13.4%, 17.1%, 17.1% and 36.6% of the respondents said that procurement processes do enhance purchase quality, enhances controls in the organization, manages possible self-interests, increases efficiency and effectiveness, supports organizational goals, and ensure that all departments are appropriately equipped.

Regarding the effect of policy/regulatory framework on organizational performance, 34.6%, 27.2%, 18.5%, 11.1% and 8.6% of the respondents explained that policy and regulatory framework influences organizational performance because it creates a level playing field, shapes the environment for decision making, acts as a guide for the employees, upholds standards of quality as well as enhance monitoring the processes respectively.

Regarding the effect of leadership and management support on organizational performance, 33.3%, 24.7%, 22.2%, 11.1% and 8.6% of the respondents felt that the procurement leadership/management does influence performance in their organization because they are the custodians of morals in an organization, they provide direction to the organization, they encourage and support the staffs, guides the junior officers to what is expected and are the main decision makers in an organization respectively.

Regarding the effect of ICT infrastructure support on organizational performance, 31%, 22%, 19%, 16% and 13% of the respondents explained that ICT; enhances efficiency, enhances monitoring and control, makes work easy, enhances communication and makes service delivery easier in that order.

Also, the researcher regressed the ratings of (the extent of satisfaction by the) public procurement contract determinants; Internal Procurement Processes, Regulatory Framework, Leadership and Management Support and ICT Infrastructure as independent variables against the rating of (the extent to which the variables do influence) performance in their organization using SPSS version 20. The output produced statistically significant results with a strong positive relationship between the study variables with coefficient of determination (R) of 0.867 and correlation coefficient (R-Square) of 0.752 respectively.

5.2.1 Hypotheses Testing

The corresponding p-value for each of the variables were less than $\alpha = 0.05$ as shown in table 11 below.

TABLE 11

P-values corresponding to each of the study variables

Independent Variables	P-value
Internal Procurement Processes	0.002
Policy and Regulatory Framework	0.008
Leadership Support	0.003
Infrastructure Support	0.001

Hypotheses

H1a: Internal procurement processes have a positive relationship with performance.

Since the obtained p-value in relation to Internal Procurement Processes was 0.002 which is less than α=0.05 the study finds no evidence to reject the alternate hypothesis. Therefore, internal procurement processes have a positive relationship with performance.

H1b: policy and regulatory frameworks have a positive relationship with organizational

performance

Since the obtained p-value in relation to policy and regulatory framework was 0.008 which is less than α=0.05 the study finds no evidence to reject the alternate hypothesis. Therefore, policy and regulatory framework have a positive relationship with organizational performance

H1c: leadership and management support has a positive relationship with organizational

performance

Since the obtained p-value in relation to policy and regulatory framework was 0.003 which is less than α=0.05 the study finds no evidence to reject the alternate hypothesis. Therefore, leadership and management support has a positive relationship with on organizational performance.

H1d: ICT infrastructure support has a positive relationship with organizational performance

Since the obtained p-value in relation to policy and regulatory framework was 0.001 which is less than α=0.05 the study finds no evidence to reject the alternate hypothesis. Therefore, ICT infrastructure support has a positive relationship with organizational performance.

5.3 Conclusions

In light of the study results, this study concludes that there is positive relationship between public procurement contract determinants and organizational performance. Regarding the effect of internal procurement processes on organizational performance, the study concludes that internal procurement processes do influence organizational performance. This is so because procurement processes do enhance purchase quality, enhances controls in the organization, manages possible self-interests, increases efficiency and effectiveness, supports organizational goals, and ensure that all departments have the purchase they adequately need in relation to budget of the organization. These findings agrees with past literatures of Porter (1985) who advanced that procurement contract life cycle management is the process of efficiently managing the contract creation, execution and analysis of the procurement process with an aim to maximizing operational and financial performance and minimizing risks. Drucker (2011) agrees with this view and points out that BPM do empower companies to align internal procurement processes to provide more value to both internal and external customers. The ultimate goal of public procurement is to provide the required goods and services in time within set budgets (Errigde and McIlroy, 2002).

Regarding the effect of policy/regulatory framework on organizational performance, the study concludes that organization policy and other regulatory frameworks do influence the performance of an organization. The policy and the set frameworks; creates a level playing field, shapes the environment for decision making, acts as a guide for the employees, upholds standards of value and quality as well as act backbone for monitoring the operational processes. This conclusion concurs with Arthur (2009) who opined that putting in place an efficient and effective contract administration mechanism is essential for the national and county government performance. Callender and Schapper (2003) held that reform to safeguard the integrity of the procurement system creasing control and audit system are essential for performance. Spiller (2008) adds that compliance with applicable regulations and policies can enhance procurement quality.

Regarding the effect of leadership and management support on organizational performance, the study concludes that leadership support does influence performance in an organization. Notably, leaders in an organization acts as custodians of morals in an organization, provides direction to the organization, cheers and motivates the staffs, guides the junior officers to what is expected and are the main decision makers in an organization. Kramer et al (2007), notes that leaders should be at the forefront when it comes to encouraging their staffs to use a particular technology. It also rhymes with the views of Were *et al.* (2012) who noted that they motivate people and are able to negotiate for resources and other support to achieve their goals. Also, Abbas and Asghar (2010) concluded that a manager must also be a leader to achieve optimum results. Furthermore, organizational leaders can alter organizational performance positively by improving the aspects that influence success of a company (Van Weele, 2006).

Regarding the effect of ICT infrastructure support on organizational performance, the study concludes that Information Communication Technology does influence organizational performance. Notably, Information Communication Technology enhances efficiency, improves monitoring and control, makes work easier, enhances communications and makes service delivery easier and faster. The conclusion agrees with Liker and Choi (2004) and Kazimoto (2013) who noted that ICT influences performance since it eases communications and understanding with suppliers as well as increases service quality and employee output. Victor (2012) said that enhancing procurement quality saves the money for the shareholders and ensures that the company has got the right inputs for better performance.

5.4 Recommendations

The study recommends that internal procurement processes for organizations should be in line with national policy regulatory framework for smooth implementation of public contracts. Harmonization of internal and external regulations allows fairness, competiveness, transparency and compliance and prevents illegal conducts in procurement.

Also, the study recommends that leadership and management support should be upheld since this is critical for organization performance. Leaders and managers should be actively involved in internal procurement process of organizations in establishing budgets, setting predetermined prices and screening the capacity of suppliers for huge public contracts.

The implementation of public contracting process should be the responsibility of procurement professionals, leadership and management of an organization. Organizations should therefore develop and uphold suitable policy and frameworks upon which the organization operates.

Further, ICT should be adopted in organizations. The support from the top management is essential since they are the key decision makers. The management should adopt appropriate ICT infrastructure support for procurement processes in bidding, technical and financial evaluation and monitoring. These can help avert possible malpractices as well as improve performance.

5.5 Further areas of research

This study sought to assess the role of internal procurement processes, policy regulatory framework, leadership and management and ICT infrastructure support on organizational performance. The study found out that internal procurement processes had the highest significance on organizational performance. Future studies should concentrate on how to enhance internal procurement processes to ensure greater organizational performance. Also, future studies should seek to unravel the best style of leadership that can enhance organizational performance in the context of public and private sector. Further, future studies should delve deeper on appropriate ICT implementation techniques to ensure maximum contribution to organizational performance. In addition, future researchers should seek to establish key aspects of policy and framework development to ensure maximum enhancement to organizational performance.

5.6 Limitation of Study

This study is limited to Nairobi County and may not directly apply to other counties due to uniqueness of Nairobi County as gate way to the Country and East African region. This is due to large population, types and nature of quality of services demanded that are benchmarked with other leading cities in the world (Murunga*et al*, 2012). Given the nature of the study, access to pertinent information on procurement contracts determinants and   implementation reports might not be provided easily. Also, conclusions may not be applicable in context of private sector.

5.7 Delimitations of the study

To ensure generalizable results were obtained, the researcher targeted all finance and procurement department officers working in the Nairobi County government to ensure diverse views were incorporated into the study. Feedback received on the Procurement Contract implementation from eight departments on goods and services provided to Nairobi residences by the County government such as road construction, garbage collection water and sewerage systems, housing, street lighting among other services are known by the respondents hence they made informed contribution to the study.

REFERENCES

Abbas, W. and Asghar, I. (2010). *The role of leadership in organizational change:* Zaria: Saad-Deen Press.

ADB, (2014). African Development Bank procurement policy, Procedure and process.

African Development Bank, (2008). *Rules and Procedures for Procurement of Goods and works*Procurement and Fiduciary Services Department May 2008 Edition, Revised July 2012.

Andras, P. and Charlton, B. G. (2005). *Management from the perspective of systems theory.* School of Computing Science, University of Newcastle.

Andrew, M. (2003). "The knowledge Link: How firms compete through Effective Contract Management", MA: Harvard Business School Press.

Apiyo, R. O, Mburu, D. K. (2014). Factors affecting procurement planning in county governments in Kenya: a case study of NairobiCity County. *International Journal of Economics, Commerce and Management* United Kingdom Vol. II, Issue 11 Page 1 ISSN 2348 0386.

Arrowsmith, S. (2010). Public procurement: Basic concepts and the coverage of procurement rules, in Public procurement relations: an introduction. EU Asia Inter University Network.

Arthur, P. (2009). An Overview of EC Policy on Public Procurement: Dorset House, New York.

Austin, R. (1996). Measuring and Managing Performance in Organizations, Dorset House, New York.

Australian, G. (2006). *Implementation of Programme and Policy Initiatives Making implementation matter.* ISBN No. 0642 809151.

Bailey, P., Farmer, D., Jessop, D., and Jones, D. (2004). *Purchasing Principles and Management,* 8th edition, Prentice Hall.

Bakos, J. Y. (1991). A Strategic Analysis of Electronic Marketplaces. *Journal MIS Quarterly - Special issue on the strategic use of information systems* Volume 15 Issue 3, Sept. 1991 Pages 295-310.

Barasa W. H. (2014). Procurement Practices Affecting Effective Public Projects Implementation in Kenya: A Case Study of Kenya Civil Aviation Authority. *European Journal of Business and Management.* ISSN 2222-1905 Vol.6, No.6.

Barclay, M., and Holderness, C. (1989). 'Private benefits from control of public corporations'. *Journal of Financial Economics* 25, 371–395.

Barney, J. and Clark, D. N. (2007). *Resource Based Theory. Creating and Sustaining Competitive Advantage:* London, Oxford University Press.

Bartik, L. (2009). Supply chain management practices in public institutions.

Bass, B. M. (1990). *Bass and Stogdill's handbook of leadership: theory research and managerial applications* 3rd edition. NY: Free Press.

BCG, (2011). High Performance organization; *Forthcoming, Journal of Financial Eco, 3-7.*

Bennett, S. (1993)."The EPI Cluster Sampling Method: A Critical Appraisal," Invited Paper, *International Statistical Institute's 49th Session.*

Blaikie, N. (1993). *Approaches to Social Enquiries,* 1st Ed. Cambridge: Policy Press.

Blaikie, N. (2000). *Designing Social Research.* 1st Ed, Polity Press, Cambridge.

Brown, L. T., Potoski, M. and VanSlyke, D. M. (2006). Managing Public Service Contracts: Aligning Values, Institutions and Markets. *Public Administration Review.* pp 323-331.

Callender, G. and Schapper, P. (2003). Public procurement Reform in Australia: a Federal-State Evaluation. International Research Study of Public Procurement, University of Bath , Bath , pp. 48-61 challenges to the public procurement law 2003 (act 663).*International Journal of construction supply chain management* Vol. 2 No. 2.

Chitkara, K. K. (2005). *Project Management - Planning, Scheduling and* Controlling – Tata McGraw Hill, New Delhi.

CIPS (2011). BPR methodologies: Methods and Tools. In J. Elzinga, T. Gulledge, and C. Lee (Eds.), *Business process engineering.*Kluwer Academic Publishers.

Cochran, W. G. (1977).*Sampling Techniques, third edition,* Wiley, New York Comparative Analysis, Industrial and Labor Relations Review, 47(1), 3-22.

Coggburn, J. D. (2003). Exploring Differences in the American States' Procurement Practices. *Journal of Public Procurement,* 3 (1), 3-28.

Cooper, D. R. and Schindler, P. S. (2006). *Business Research Method,* 9th ed. Boston: McGraw Hill. Irwin.

Cortina, A. (2008). Cronbach alpha:An examination of theory and applications. *Journal of applied psychology, vol. 78,* 98-104.

Del, O. (2008). The Legal theory of competitive bidding for government contracts 37 P.C.L 237; Cibic and Nash PP537-592 of purchasing Vol 22.

Dew, N. (2008). 'Cookies for real world: assessing the potential of RFID for contractor monitoring, *Journal of Public Procurement*, Vol. 8, No 1, pp.98–129.

Drucker, P. (2011). Practice of Management. *Purchasing Journal,* Vol. 6, No 2, pp. 98–129.

Ellram, L.M. (1995). Partnering pitfalls and success factors, *International Journal of Purchasing and Material management* 31(2).

Eriksson, P. and Kovalainen, A. (2008). *Qualitative Methods in Business Research, 1st ed,* SAGE Publications Ltd., London. Future Prospects", Public Procurement Law Review, Vol. 1 No.1, pp.28-39.

Ferris, J. and Graddy, E. (1986). Contracting out: For what? With whom? *Public Administration Review* 46:332–44.

Flowers, P. (2009). *Research Philosophies- Importance and Relevance.* London: Cranfield Scool of Management.

Fradkov, M. (2004). "State Procurement to reach 40% of 2004 Budget Expenses." *The Russia Journal Daily.*

Gavrea, C., Ilies, L. and Stegerean, R. (2011). Determinants of Organizational performance: The case of Romania.

Goleman, D. (2004). What makes a leader? Harvard *Business Review*, Special Issue – Inside the Minds of the Leader pp. 82-91.

Gordon, S. B., Zemansky, S. D. and Sekwat, A. (2000). The Public Purchasing Profession Revisited. *Journal of Public Budgeting, Accounting and Financial Management,* 12 (2): 248-271.

Grant, M. R. (2001). The Resource Based Theory of Competitive Advantage: Implementation of Strategic formulation.

Gul, H. (2010). Modernizing public procurement and creating an independent public Procurement regulatory authority. Law transition online.

Gunningham, N., and Kagan, R. A. (2005). Regulation and business behavior. *Law and Policy*, (27), 213-18.

Hagans, C. (2013). Livelihoods, land-use and public transport: Opportunities for poverty reduction and risks of splintering urbanism in Nairobi's Spatial Plans.

Hatch, M. J and Cunliffe, A. L. (2006). *Organisation Theory.* 2nd ed. Oxford: Oxford University Press.

Hawthorne, M. (2013). Management Theories and Concepts at the Workplace, Demand Media, Chron.

Hui, W. S., Othman, R. O., Normah, O., Rahman, R. A., and Haron, N. H. (2011). Procurement issues in Malaysia. *International Journal of Public Sector Management,* 24(6), 567-593.

Imperato, G. L. (2005). Corporate crime, responsibility, compliance and governance. *Journal of Health Care Compliance,* 7(3), 11-19.

James, K. and Vinnicombe, S. (2002). "Acknowledging the Individual in the Researcher", in Partington, D. (ed). *Essential Skills for Management Research.* 1st Ed. London: Sage Publications.

Jensen, M. C., and Meckling, W. (1976). Theory of the Firm: Managerial Behavior, Agency Costs and Ownership Structure. *Journal of Financial Economics,* 3: 305-60.

Jiang, B. and Qureshi, A. (2006). *Research on Outsourcing results:* Current Literature and future opportunities, Management Decision. Vol.44 No.1 pp44-55.

Johnson, B. and Christensen, L. (2010). *Educational research: Quantitative, Qualitative and Mixed Approaches.* London: Sage.

Jordan and Young (2008).Top Management Support. *International Journal of Project.*

Karanja, G. J. and Ng'ang'a, N. E. (2014). Factors Influencing Implementation of Integrated Financial Management Information System in Kenya Government Ministries. *Research Journal of Finance and Accounting* ISSN 2222-1697 Vol.5, No.7.

Kariuki, C., and Nzioki, N. (2010).The Management of Corporate Real Estate Assets in Kenya. FIG Congress 2010 Facing the Challenges – Building the Capacity Sydney, Australia, 11-16 .

Kavua, K. B. and Ngugi, K. (2014). Determinants of Procurement Performance of Rural Electrification Projects. *European Journal of Business Management,* 1 (11), 361-377.

Kazimoto, P. (2013). Analysis of conflict management and leadership for organizational change. *International Journal of Research In Social Sciences* Vol. 3, No.1. ISSN 2307-227X.

Kiama, P.G (2014). Factors Affecting Implementation of Public Procurement Act in SACCO Societies in Kenya.*International Journal of Academic Research in Business and Social Sciences* Vol. 4, No. 2 ISSN: 2222-6990.

Kothari, C. (2004). *Research Methodology: Methods and Techniques*, 2nd Ed. Delhi: New Age International Limited.

Kraaijenbrink, J., Spender, C., and Groen, A. (2010). The resource –based view: A review and assessment of its critiques. *Journal of Management*, 36(5), pp.364-381.

Kramer, J. K. (2007). The Role of the Information and Communication Technology Sector in Expanding Economic Opportunities,Local Governance and Accountability Series Paper No. 113.

Lan, Z.G., Riley, L. and Cayer, J. N. (2005). 'How can local Government Become and Employer of Choice for Technical professionals?',*Review of Public Administration*, Vol25, No.3, pp. 225-242.

Laratta, R. (2009). "Autonomy and accountability in social services nonprofits: Japan and UK", *Social Enterprise Journal*, Vol. 5 Iss: 3, pp.259 – 281.

Lardenoije, E. J., Van Raaij, E. M., and Van Weele, A. J. (2005). Performance Management Models and Purchasing: Relevance Still Lost. *Researches in Purchasing and Supply Management, the 14th IPSERA Conference, (pp. 687-97). Arch amps.*

Lee, H. L., Padmanabhan, V., and Whang, S. (1997). Information distortion in a supply chain: The bullwhip, *Management Science*, 43(4).

Lee, S. Y. (2007). Impacts of Organization Resources on Agency Performance.

Li, S., Rao, S. S., Ragunathan, T. S., and Ragunathan, B. (2005). Development and validation of a measurement instrument for studying supply chain management practices, *Journal of Operations Management* 23(6).

Liker, J. K. and Choi, T. Y. (2004). Building deep supplier relationships, *Harvard Business Review*, 82 (12).

Macharia, J. (2009). Factors affecting E-Commerce Adoption: Nairobi, United States International University.

Maiyo, P. (2009). Irregularities in undertaking procurement practices in public institutions. *Journal Management* 0263-7863.

Mamiro, R. G. (2010). Value for Money, The Limping Pillar in Public Procurement. *Tanzania Procurement Journal*, 4 -5.

March, G. J and Sutton, I. R. (2015). Organizational performance as a dependent variable.

Masterman, J. W. E. (1996). *Building Procurement Systems: An Introduction*. London: E and FN Spon.

Mclvor, R. T. (2000). 'A Practical Framework for Understanding the outsourcing Process', Supply Chain management: *An International Journal,* Vol.5.No.1, pp.22-36.

Minahan, T. (2007). Get Real: The Secret to Supply Risk Management. *Journal of Business Logistics.*Vol. 21, No. 2, pp. 1-16.

Monczka, R. M., Morgan, J., Trent, R. J., Handfield, B. (1998). Purchasing and Supply Chain Management, South-Western, Cincinnati, OH.,*International Thomson publishing, and United States of America.*

Mugambi, W. K., Theuri, S. F. (2014). The Challenges Encountered By County Government In Kenya During Budget Preparation. *IOSR Journal of Business and Management* (IOSR-JBM) e-ISSN: 2278-487X, p-ISSN: 2319-7668. Volume 16, Issue 2. pp 128-134.

Muge, P. (2009). Procurement practices in public institutions in Kenya.

Mugenda, A. and Mugenda, A. O. (2003). *Quantitative and Qualitative Approaches.* Nairobi Kenya: African Centre for Technological Studies.

Mugenda, M. A. (2003). *Research Methods, Quantitative and Qualitative Approaches.* Nairobi: Acts Press.

Murdoch, J. and Hughes, W. (2000*). Construction Contract: Law and Management*: 3rd Edition. London: EandFN Spon.

Nadiope, M. (2005). *"Effects of Contract Management Methods of Donor funded projects on the construction Industry in Uganda", Final Year project, Department of Civil Engineering.*Kyambogo University (unpublished).

Nicol, W. (2003). "Mainstreaming the Procurement Function into the Public Expenditure Policy and Effectiveness Dialogue." Paper presented at the World Bank Roundtable, Paris, France, January 22-23.

Ntayi, J. M., Byabashaija, S., Eyaa, S., Ngoma, M., and Muliira, A. (2010). Social Cohesion, Groupthink and Ethical Behavior of Public Procurement Officers. *Journal of Public Procurement, Vol. 10, No. 1, pp. 68 – 92.*

Nzau, A. and Njeru, A. (2014). Factors affecting procurement performance of public universities in Nairobi County. *International Journal of Social Sciences and Project Planning Management.*1 (3), 147-156.21 No.1, pp.49-73.

Odhiambo, W., and Kamau, P. (2003). Public Procurement: Lessons from Kenya, Tanzania and Uganda, OECD Development Centre Working Paper No. 208.

Ongore, O. V. and K'Obonyo, O .P. (2011). Effects of Selected Corporate Governance Characteristics on Firm Performance: Empirical Evidence from Kenya. *International Journal of Economics and Financial Issues* Vol. 1, No. 3, pp.99-122 ISSN: 2146-4138.

Orodho, A .J. (2009). Research Method Overview, *International Journal of Economics and Financial Issues* Vol. 4, No. 2, pp.89-112.

Paul, S. (2011). Procurement policies in public corporations. *Journal of Purchasing.* 33(4), pp. 26-45.

Pegnato, J. A. (2003). Assessing Federal Procurement Reform: Has the Procurement Pendulum Stopped Swinging? *Journal of Public Procurement*, 3 (2).

Porter, E. (1980). *"Competitive Strategy"*, The Free Press, New York.

Porter, M. (1985). *Procurement strategies: A relationship Based approach*, Blackwell Publishing, Oxford.

Posner, R. A. (1993). "The New Institutional Economics Meets Law and Economics," *Journal of Institutional and Theoretical Economics*, 149 .pp73-87.

Rahim, A. (2010). *Managing conflict in organizations*. Library of congress catalog number: 2010017602. ISBN : 978-1-4128-1456-1.

Raymond, J. (2008) "Benchmarking in public procurement", Benchmarking: *An International Journal*, 15 (6), 782 – 793.

Raymond, J. (2005). *Management Information Systems*, 6th Ed. New Jersey: Prentice Hall.

Richard, P J and Devinney, T and Yip, G and Johnson, G (2009) Measuring organizational performance: towards methodological best practice. Journal of Management, 35 (3). pp. 718-804.

Roos, G. and Roos, J. (1997). Measuring your company's intellectual performance. *Journal of Long Range Planning*, 30(3), pp. 325 - 567.

Rotich, K. C, and Ngahu, S. (2015). Factors affecting budget utilization Kericho county government in Kenya: *International Journal of Economics, Commerce and Management United Kingdom* Vol. III, Issue 6, *Page 510.*

Sagepub. (2014). *Research Philosophies and Qualitative Interviews*. [Online] Available at http://www.sagepub.com/upm-data/43179_2.pdf [Accessed 12th July, 2014].

Salem, H. (2003). Organizational Performance Management and Measurement.

Sanders, R. N., Locke, A., Moore, B. C., and Autry, W. C. (2007). A Multidimensional Framework for Understanding Outsourcing Arrangements. *The journal of Supply* chain *management: A Global review of Purchasing and supply,* pp3-15.

Sauber, M. H., McSurely, H. B., RaoV. M. (2008). "Developing supply chain management program: a competency model", *Quality Assurance in Education,* Vol. 16 Iss: 4, pp.375 - 391.

Saunders, M. (2003). *Researcher Methods for Business Students.* Pretoria: Pearson Education.

Saunders, M., Lewis, P. and Thornhill, A. (2007). *Research Methods for Business Students,* 4th ed, Prentice Hall Financial Times, Harlow.

Sekaran, U. and Bougie, R. (2010). *Research Method for business: A skill Building Approach,*5th ed. Hoboken, N.J/Chichester: John Wiley and Sons.

Sekaran, U. (2005). *Research Methods for Business, a Skill Building Approach* (4[th]ed.).

Sharma, M. K, Jain, S. (2013). Leadership Management: Principles, Models and Theories. *Global Journal of Management and Business Studies.*Vol 3, No 3, pp. 309-318.

Smith, R. and Conway, G. (1993). Organization of Procurement in Government Departments and their Agencies. London: HM Treasury Consultancy and Inspection Services Division.

Spiller, P. T. (2008). An Institutional Theory of Public Contracts: Regulatory Implications. Working paper. University of California, Berkeley and NBER.

Steinberg, R., (2003). Strategies for successful Government E-Procurement, Gartner Inc., *Journal of Business Logistics,* Vol. 21 No.2. *Supply chain management journal.* Vol 22.

Swinney, R. and Netessin, S. (2007). Long-Term Contracts under the Threat of Supplier Default.

Tan, K. S., Chong, S. C., and Uchenna, C. E. (2009)."Factors influencing the adoption of internet-based ICTs: evidence from Malaysian SMEs", *International Journal of Management and Enterprise Development.*

Thai, K. V. (2004). *Introduction to Public Procurement (IPP).*Washington D.C.: National Institute of Government Purchasing (NIGP).

The Aqua Group (2001). *Tenders and Contract for Building-* 3rd. Edition. London: Blackwell Science.

Thomson, P. (2007). Supplier selection methods in public institutions.*Journal of purchasing.*

TOG,2009. *A practical Guide to Contract Management.*

Trevor, L. B, Matthew, P. and David, M. S. (2006). Managing Public Service Contracts: Aligning Values, Institutions, and Markets. *Public Administration Review.*

Upadhaya, B., Munir, R., and Blount, Y. (2014). Association between Performance Measurement Systems and Organisational Effectiveness. International Journal of Operations and Production Management, 34(7), 2-2.

Van Weele, A. J. (2006). *Purchasing and Supply Chain Management*: Analysis, Strategy, Planning and Practice, (4th Ed.). Australia: Thomson.

Victor, A. (2012). Challenges affecting procurement practices in public corporations. *International journal* Vol. 28-33.

Wenyang, Y. (2005). *Database Security Threats and Counter Measures*. University of Washington.

William, S. 2009. *Operations Management*, 10th edition, McGraw –Hill/Irwin.

Williamson, O. E. (2002). The lens of contract: Private ordering. *American Economic Review* 92(2): 438-443.

Williamson, O. E. (2000). The New Institutional Economics: Taking Stock, Looking Ahead. *Journal of Economic Literature, Vol38 595-613.*

World Bank, (2007). *World Development Report 2007: Development and the Next Generation,* Oxford University Press, New York, NY.

Wymer, S., Regan, E. (2005). Factors influencing e-commerce adoption and use by small and medium businesses, Electronic *Markets, Vol. 15* No.4, pp.438-53.

Yukl, G. (2002). *Leadership in organisations* (5th ed.). Upper Saddle River, NJ: Prentice-Hall.

Zaleznik, A. (2004). 'Managers and leaders: are they different?'*Harvard Business Review,* Special Issue – Inside the Minds of the Leader, pp. 74-81.

Zubcic, J., and Sims, R. (2011). Examining the link between enforcement activity and corporate compliance by Australian companies and the implications for regulators. *International Journal of Law and Management,* 53(4), 299-308.

APPENDICES

Appendix I: Data Collection Instrument Questionnaire

Dear Respondent,

I am Karungani Walter Philip, a Master of Business Administration (Procurement and Supply Chain Management) student at KCA University. I am undertaking a dissertation on "Effect of Procurement Contract determinants on the Organizational Performance: A case of Nairobi county". The purpose of the study is simply academic (for this course only).

Kindly, I request for your time to fill this questionnaire objectively and exhaustively. I assure that the information you will provide will be used for academic consumptions only and will be treated with utmost confidentiality. The instruction for filling the questionnaire is availed for each question.

Part A: General information

1.   Gender: Male   [   ] Female   [   ]
2.   How long have you worked in the organization?

        Below 2 years [ ]   2-6 years [ ]   7-10 years [ ] Above 10 years [ ]

3.   How long have you worked in the current position?

Below 5 years [ ]   5-10 years   [ ]   10-15 years   [ ]   15-20 years [ ]

4.   Please indicate your highest level of education:

PhD   [ ]   Masters [ ]   Bachelors [ ]   Diploma [ ] Certificate [ ]

Section B: Internal Procurement Processes

5.   To what extent does the presence of Internal Procurement Processes affect Organizational Performance?

        To a very great extent   [ ]
        To a great extent   [ ]

Neutral   [ ]
To a little extent   [ ]
To no extent   [ ]

6.   What is the key role of Internal Procurement Processes in relation to organizational performance?
……
……………………………………………………………………………………………

7.   What is your level of agreement with the following statements that relate to effects of Internal Procurement Regulations on Organizational Performance? (1-Strongly agree, 2-Strongly agree, 3-Neutral,4- Disagree, 5 Strongly Disagree)

Statement	1	2	3	4	5
My company has Internal Procurement Processes					
The Internal Procurement Processes are responsible for Organizational Performance					
Internal Procurement Processes do not say anything about Organizational Performance					
The presence of Internal Procurement Processes is positively associated with Organizational Performance					

8.   How do you think the presence of Internal Procurement Processes affect Organizational performance?
……
………………………………………………………………………………………………

Section C: Policy and Regulatory Framework

9.   In your opinion, what need for policy and regulatory framework in your organization?
……
………………………………………………………………………………………………

10.   To what extent does the independence of Policy and Regulatory Framework affect Organization Performance?
            To a very great extent [ ]
            To a great extent   [ ]
            Neutral   [ ]
            To a little extent   [ ]
            To no extent   [ ]

11.   What is your level of agreement with the following statements that relate to independence of Policy and Regulatory Framework effect on Organizational Performance? (1-Strongly agree, 2- Strongly agree, 3-Neutral,4- Disagree, 5 Strongly Disagree)

Statement	1	2	3	4	5
Policy and Regulatory Framework play a key role in determining					

Organizational Performance					
Policy and Regulatory Framework is involved in the Organizational Performance					
Policy and Regulatory Framework enhance Organizational Performance					

12.	How do you think the independence of Policy and Regulatory Framework affects Organizational Performance?

………………………………………………………………………………………………

………………………………………………………………………………………

Section D: Leadership and Management Support

13.	In your opinion, why is the Leadership and Management Support of procurement endeavors important in your organization

………………………………………………………………………………………………………

………………………………………………………………………………………

14.	To what extent does Leadership and Management Support affect Organizational Performance?

To a very great extent [ ]
To a great extent   [ ]
To a moderate extent [ ]
To a little extent   [ ]
To no extent   [ ]

15.	What is your level of agreement with the following statements that relate to effect of Leadership and Management Support on Organizational Performance? (1-Strongly agree, 2-Strongly agree, 3-Neutral,4- Disagree, 5 Strongly Disagree)

Statement	1	2	3	4	5
Commitment and support from Leadership and Management Support plays a key role in influencing the success in almost any initiative within an organization					
Business vision positively influence Organizational Performance					
Leadership and Management Support staffing in the Organizational Performance					
The essence of commitment from Leadership and Management support in decision-making process					
Leadership and Management Support for external expertise which positively influence the Organizational Performance					
The presence of Leadership and Management support is positively associated with Organizational Performance					

The Leadership and Management Support is involved in the Organizational Performance					

16.   How do you think the Leadership and Management Support affect the Organizational Performance?

....

....

Section E: ICT Infrastructure Support

17.   To what extent do you rate the robustness of the ICT Infrastructure in your organization
        To a very great extent [ ]
        To a great extent   [ ]
        To a moderate extent [ ]
        To a little extent   [ ]
        To no extent   [ ]

18.   To what extent does the ICT Infrastructure affect the Organizational Performance?
        To a very great extent [ ]
        To a great extent   [ ]
        To a moderate extent [ ]
        To a little extent   [ ]
        To no extent   [ ]

19.   What is your level of agreement with the following statements that relate to ICT Infrastructure Support and the effect on the Organizational Performance? (1-Strongly agree, 2-Strongly agree, 3-Neutral, 4- Disagree, 5 Strongly Disagree)

Statement	1	2	3	4	5
The faster a county develops, the more likely it will embrace Organizational Performance evaluation					
Increased costs due to development hinder Organizational Performance					
The increased size leads to increased bureaucracy which may hinder Organizational Performance					
Large counties have a higher probability of adopting Organizational Performance evaluation					

20.   How do you think ICT Infrastructure Support affect the Organizational Performance?

....

....

Measurement of performance

21.   In a Likert scale (between 1-10), please rate the importance of each of the following aspects of an organization, and the extent to which they influence organizational performance (attainment of organizational goals and objectives).

Aspect of the Organization	Rate the importance of each aspect in an organization (Between 1-10)	Extent to which each influence organization's performance (Between 1-10)
1 Internal Procurement Processes		
2 Policy Regulatory Framework		
3 Leadership and Management Support		
4 ICT Infrastructure Support		

22. In a scale of 1-10, rate the extent to which procurement contract determinants as Internal Procurement Processes, Policy Regulatory Framework, Leadership and Management Support, ICT Infrastructure Support, have influenced your company's BSC over the last 1 year.

Financial measure (BSC)	Rating (Between 1-10)
1 Financial measure	
2 Customer Satisfaction	
3 Internal organizational processes	
4 Employee needs – learning and development	

Thank you for participating